BizBreak

Weekly Reminders for the Workplace

Mark Slomka

HORIZON BOOKS

CAMP HILL, PENNSYLVANIA

HORIZON BOOKS

3825 Hartzdale Drive, Camp Hill, Pennsylvania 17011
www.cpi-horizon.com
www.christianpublications.com

BizBreak: Weekly Reminders for the Workplace
ISBN: 0-88965-189-2
LOC Control Number: 00-131979
© 2000 by Horizon Books
All rights reserved
Printed in the United States of America

00 01 02 03 04 5 4 3 2 1

With Love and in Honor of

My parents, Bruce and Arlene Slomka—your love and example prepared me for the faith I treasure.

My wife, Carol—your loving commitment reflects a beauty that comes from Jesus and makes me a better man.

My daughters: Alison, Catherine, Bethany and Danielle—your love, along with your laughter and hugs, reminds me of the gift and honor God has given me to be called your dad.

The church family and staff of Mount Soledad Presbyterian Church—there can be no greater blessing bestowed upon any pastor than to be called to serve you.

With Thanks to:

Karen O'Connor Flowers—this book would never have been published without your encouragement and legwork; *the many who subscribe to BIZBREAK*—your willingness to read a weekly devotion provided me with the challenge and opportunity to write; and to those whose faith, leadership and example has shaped my soul—*Ed Beach, Jack Hayford, David Mac-*

Innes, Jim Rueb, Len Sunukjian and the late *David Watson.*

Finally, thank you to the staff at Horizon Books: Your desire to publish this book by an "unknown" is a gift and a blessing to me.

CONTENTS

Foreword ix
Introduction: Please Read First 1

Part One: Confident

Week One:
   Confident in Christ's Rule 9
Week Two:
   Confident in God's Promises 13
Week Three:
   Confident in the Person of Jesus 17
Week Four:
   Confident in Our Coming King 21

Part Two: Purposeful

Week One:
   God Is Purposeful 29
Week Two:
   You Have a Purpose 33
Week Three:
   You Have a Purpose for Such a Time as This 37
Week Four:
   Discover Your Purpose 41

Part Three: Devoted

Week One:
   Devoted to Worship (Part 1) 47
Week Two:
   Devoted to Worship (Part 2) 51
Week Three:
   Devoted to Prayer (Part 1) 55
Week Four:
   Devoted to Prayer (Part 2) 59

Week Five:
   Devoted to Prayer (Part 3)...............................63
Week Six:
   Devoted to God's Word......................................67
Week Seven:
   Devoted to Giving 71

Part Four: Spirit-Filled

Week One:
   Filled with the Holy Spirit 77
Week Two:
   The Testimony of the Holy Spirit 83
Week Three:
   You Shall Receive Power 87
Week Four:
   A Sign of the Spirit 91

Part Five: Vibrant

Week One:
   A Man Made New 97
Week Two:
   Your Life Is Destined to Be Fruitful 103
Week Three:
   Obedience Is Our Cornerstone 107
Week Four:
   Build a Life-Giving Church 111

Part Six: Upright

Week One:
   The Uniqueness of Christian Integrity 117
Week Two:
   The Hallmarks of Integrity.............................121
Week Three:
   Ten Steps to Christian Integrity....................125
Week Four:
   Sexual Integrity (Part 1)...............................129

Week Five:
　Sexual Integrity (Part 2)..............................133
Week Six:
　Integrity Values Repentance.........................137

Part Seven: Committed

Week One:
　Are You Prepared?......................................145
Week Two:
　Faith without Commitment Is NO Faith at All..........149
Week Three:
　A Singular Passion 153
Week Four:
　Committed to Serve, Not Rule....................157
Week Five:
　Committed to Seeing God's Work in Your Work 163

Part Eight: Empowered

Week One:
　Be Strong in God's Power..............................169
Week Two:
　The Promise of Power 173
Week Three:
　God's Strength for Daily Living....................177
Week Four:
　Empowered Endurance 181

Part Nine: World-Changing

Week One:
　A Person of Impact 187
Week Two:
　Nothing Is Impossible for God....................191
Week Three:
　Never Underestimate Your Impact 195
Week Four:
　There Is Nothing Dull about Jesus 199

Week Five:
A Love That Wins Hearts...203

Part Ten: Victorious

Week One:
That Was Then . . . This Is Now 209
Week Two:
Defeating Intimidation (Part 1)...................................213
Week Three:
Defeating Intimidation (Part 2)...................................217
Week Four:
Closing in on God's Promises.......................................221
Week Five:
Live in the Authority God Gave You 225
Week Six:
Beware of Complacency! 231
Week Seven:
Fidelity and Unity Are Inseparable..............................235
Week Eight:
Your Battles Are the Lord's 239

Endnotes 243

A foreword to a book is to put you in touch with the theme, as well as to give you a sense of acquaintance with the author, if you've not met. So let me be direct: I like Mark Slomka. I think you will too. And I'm bold to say so, because even if you never experience the pleasure of a personal meeting (or acquaintance, as I've been privileged to gain), you're on the brink of an encounter with someone very genuine right here and now.

I got to know Mark through his involvement in a series of week-long, small group intensive "Consultations" for pastors. These are highly interactive, candid and transparent sessions that I conduct each month at the Jack W. Hayford School of Pastoral Nurture. By the time you read this, upwards of a thousand men and women (almost entirely senior pastors) will have participated in one of our consultations. Mark was at the first one.

It wasn't long before I discovered things about him that now occasion my boldness in recommending his thoughts and ministry to you. He is, like I said, genuine: a genuinely hungry-for-God kind of leader who is genuinely professional, but genuinely convinced that the most genuine "genuineness" goes deeper than skill, becomes brighter than the best brain and touches and transforms the heart. Genuinely.

Yet make no mistake in supposing the genuineness of this man's heart is a substitute for a very clear head. I've found Mark to be a capable thinker with a focus on sound theology and careful exposition of God's Word. But neither seem to get in the way of his being a "right here, in-touch-with-people, personal and practical" communicator.

The motive and structure for this book say it all.

The writer's motive shines. He's obviously interested in more than selling ideas. Mark is providing thoughtful, pragmatic people with the stuff of a life-changing, mind-transforming encounter with God's truth and God's Spirit. He's unapologetically proposing personal spiritual change and growth, but in a nonreligious, unpredictable way that makes points that nail truth home—and build you up.

He's also structured the material in bite-sized, week-to-week (or day-to-day if you want) chunks. The format not only makes the material here more palatable, but it seems to me it will make it even more credible—that is, believable—so that people like you and me can actually get a lasting grip on what's being served up.

So step up to the plate: not on the baseball diamond, but to a table of truth with a rich menu—

none of it "fatty stuff." Here is meat for men and women. And when you push back from the table a few chapters from now, I guarantee you'll be stronger at all the points where life really counts.

And I think you'll like Mark in the way I do because at the bottom line of his life, teaching and writing, he brings you to know and love Jesus Christ more, and you will come to understand Him and His way better.

Jack W. Hayford
Chancellor/Pastor
The King's College and Seminary
The Church on the Way

Please Read First

I regularly meet followers of Jesus who are faithful in gathering for worship, consistent in their private devotions and generous in the giving of their time, talent and treasure, and earnest in their desire to serve Him.

Yet many feel frustrated and disheartened by the compromises they perceive themselves to be making at work. Their painful confessions echo the words of Paul: "I am not practicing what I would like to do, but I am doing the very thing I hate" (Romans 7:15). Their discouragement is compounded when they recognize that God also intends their vocations to be the public and visible location of their witness and service to Him. The result is a series of spiritual defeats, ranging from the trivial to the significant, that smothers their witness and chips away at their identity as men and women of God, their awareness of God's presence, their recognition of God's love and strength and their expectation that God desires to use them to impact lives at work, at church and at home with the person and power of Jesus Christ.

I do not think that our vocations are inherently antithetical to our commitment to Jesus so much as they are indifferent. The reality for most of us is that our Christian faith is tolerated to the extent that it is not intrusive or intolerant. Very few of us labor in work environments that proactively encourage, remind and reward a steadfast commitment to Jesus that is expressed through our vocations. Thus, many people apply their strength, ingenuity and creativity fifty-plus hours each week for decades toward something that they erroneously perceive as fundamentally disconnected from what matters most to God. Amidst the maelstrom of daily urgencies, the absence of Christian fellowship and the silence of biblical encouragement, it becomes easier to live as though we forget God's abiding presence and call rather than remember. Herein lies a fundamental problem. . . .

Remember is one of the most important, and also one of the most skipped over, words in Scripture. It occurs in its Hebrew and Greek forms over 250 times to clearly reveal:

- the immediacy and the intensity of God's love for us;
- the passionate exercise of His sovereign rule on our behalf;
- the complete expression of His unconditional grace;
- the attentiveness of His shepherding care and provision; and

- ❦ the vindication of His justice over evil and sin.

Remember is also used to exhort and encourage God's people

- ❦ to recognize with reverence and awe His might, His rule and His steadfast love;
- ❦ to recall His saving work on our behalf;
- ❦ to realize our obligation to obey His commands;
- ❦ to reflect daily on the reality of God's presence and our faithfulness to Him; and
- ❦ to repent when our thoughts, words and deeds tragically reflect that we have "forgotten" Him.

Remember discloses God's desire to have a relationship with us that is personal, immediate, substantial and faithful. This relationship is not theoretical, mystical, virtual or mysterious. Because God "remembers," He contends for an authentic relationship with us so that the benefits of His presence may make a tangible impact on our daily lives. God expects us to live so that our thoughts, words and deeds indicate that we are joyfully and gratefully cognizant of this precious relationship we share. God expects our fidelity just as husbands and wives expect their beloved to live in a manner that actively honors and treasures the uniqueness of their marriage relationship. Just as a marriage is jeopardized the moment its partners begin to "forget" one another, so too our relationship with God is undermined when we cease to live as though we remember Him. In short, God tells us that He will remember us always and He calls us to do likewise.

> Remember these things, O Jacob, and Is-
> rael, for you are My servant; I have formed
> you, you are My servant, O Israel, you will
> not be forgotten by Me. (Isaiah 44:21)

Five years ago I began writing a series of letters that I called *BizBreak—Weekly Reminders for the Workplace*. These reflections were originally written for men and e-mailed weekly in order to arrive at their desks on Wednesday. Their simple purpose was and remains to remind men that they belong to Jesus Christ in order that they may show themselves a man of God (see 1 Corinthians 7:23; cf. 1 Kings 2:2).

Most of the men who receive these letters have a passion for Christ's fullness and a sincere desire to serve Him. I found that they did not need to be pushed—only gently nudged toward the riches and resources of God's grace and presence. I am gratified that over the last five years I have seen God use these weekly reminders to encourage, challenge, comfort and release men

- to expect God's gracious visitation while at work;
- to see kingdom purpose in their market-place responsibilities;
- to recognize demonic advocacy and trust that the battle belongs to the Lord;

- to be confident in the Holy Spirit's presence, fullness and counsel regardless of circumstance;
- to utilize the rich resources of worship, prayer and Scripture while at work; and
- to experience congruity in their relationship with Jesus as they move through their own spheres of work, church and home.

I hope that they may do the same for you. . .

How to use this book . . .

These weekly reflections are not intended to replace a habit of regular Bible reading and prayer time with God. Instead, I think they will serve you best if you use them as a midweek reminder. Each chapter is purposely brief in order to be read quickly but I have tried to avoid a trite, pat, shallow or trivial presentation of biblical themes and issues. Those who find these readings most helpful schedule a twenty-minute appointment with themselves midway through their workweek in order to read, reflect and pray. Others have found it helpful to follow up their private "appointments" with a regular lunch or breakfast meeting with other believers to discuss and apply the week's reflection.

A quick note about language . . .

My use of personal pronouns in this book is overwhelmingly masculine because I have written these reflections with men as my primary target. The truth is that most of the themes and issues presented here are common to both men and women who hunger to be found faithful.

My prayer is that you will be blessed and encouraged
To live for Christ,
To be responsive to His presence and
    leadership in your midst,
To be confident in the counsel
    of His Word and
To be challenged by His clear and clarion call,

Give heed to yourself and keep your soul diligently, so that you do not forget the things which your eyes have seen and they do not depart from your heart all the days of your life. . . . Remember the day you stood before the LORD your God. (Deuteronomy 4:9-10)

PART ONE:

Confident

For a person to achieve all that is demanded of him he must be confident in the God who is great than he is. Then he will discover that confidence is little more than faith under pressure.

Confident in Christ's Rule

*For a child has been born to us, a son
has been given to us;
And the government has been resting on
His shoulders;
And His name has been called Wonderful
Counselor, Mighty God,
Eternal Father, Prince of Peace.
(Isaiah 9:6, author's paraphrase)*

ere begins the first lesson: Mind your verbs. Your past, present and future depend on them.

Here begins the second lesson: The perfect tense derives its name from the Latin *perfectus*, meaning "carried through to the end, complete." The perfect tense denotes action that is completed and over with, or a state already achieved and complete.

Here begins the third lesson: The tense of choice for Isaiah is perfect, not future. He is so convicted about the certainty of God's Word that he writes about the future as if it were the past.

This can only mean one thing—the future is history. Therefore . . .

Trend prophets,
   Demographic augurs,
      Economic forecasters,
         Environmental clairvoyants and
            Geopolitical seers
               Take heed . . .

Worriers,
   Pessimists,
      Fretters,
         Optimists and the
            Fearful
               Take note . . .

The future is history.

Fate,
   Whim,
      Luck,
         Chance and
            Kismet
               Are each rendered impotent because

The future is history.

We will beware of any speculative vision of the future that fails to:
   give Jesus preeminence;
      reckon with His righteous judgment;
         recognize His sovereign rule;
         take courage in His covenant-destiny; and

be assured by the certainty of His promises.

The future is history.

Faith recognizes that the future is unknown.
Faith rejects the notion that the future is uncertain.

The future is history because we are certain
that Christ completely holds the future.

What can be added to it?
He is the First and the Last.
What can be taken away from it?
He is the Beginning and the End.
What can elude His rule?
He is the Lord Almighty.
He is the One Who Was
and Who Is and
Who Is to Come.

In Jesus Christ the future is history.

What Isaiah saw prophetically we see histori-
cally—but not more completely than he did. Otherwise why would we be drawn to his prophecy
season after season? Isaiah beheld the certainty of
God's future in Christ prophetically revealed to his
present. He strategically oriented his life around
God's "historic future" and called Israel to do the
same. God summons us to "back into" the future
like the rower who goes forward while looking
backward toward a reference point on the horizon.

Our reference point is the promises of God.
Our destination is God's promised future.

Until next week . . .

Confident in God's Promises

After the death of Moses the servant of the LORD, the LORD said to Joshua son of Nun, Moses' aide: "Moses my servant is dead. Now then, you and all these poeple, get ready to cross the Jordan River into the land I am about to give to them—to the Israelites. I will give you every place where you set your foot, as I promised Moses. Your territory will extend from the desert to Lebanon, and from the great river, the Euphrates—all the Hittite country—to the Great Sea on the west. No one will be able to stand up against you all the days of your life. As I was with Moses, so I will be with you; I will never leave you nor forsake you.

"Be strong and courageous, because you will lead these people to inherit the land I swore to their forefathers to give them. Be strong and very courageous. Be careful to obey all the law my servant Moses gave you; do not turn from it to the right or to the left, that you may be

*successful wherever you go. Do not let
this Book of the Law depart from your
mouth; meditate on it day and night, so
that you may be careful to do everything
written in it. Then you will be prosperous
and successful." (Joshua 1:1-8, NIV)*

od's promises—His expectations and
dreams for us—are a gift and resource
that sets us apart from the animal kingdom. God's promises cannot be deduced with the
powers of our intellect nor apprehended through
the insight of our intuition. They are revealed by
His Spirit and become embedded in our longings.
When God's promises overtake us we can no longer conceive of our future without their fulfillment.

One of the tragedies of our times is that many
Christians do not expect God to promise them anything except life after death. We have lost all sense
that we are children with a purposed destiny because our God and Father has spoken over us before we were ever born. God wants us to enjoy our
salvation *and the fulfillment of His purposes for us*.

I recognize that this is difficult to embrace because:

- Many of us are cautious. We have been
  hurt, and the more frequently promises
  have been broken, the more difficult this
  subject will be.
- Many of us are trapped by a legalism.
  Somewhere along the way we picked up

the mistaken notion that says you have to be some kind of mystic or super-spiritual person to be in touch with God's promises.

🕸 Many of us are unsure of the timing of God's promises. We fear the commitments that trust requires—patience, fortitude and a willingness to risk.

Dear ones, beware of the human desire to domesticate your faith into something that is controllable, predictable and acceptable to your well-reasoned future. Faith wants to be set free to walk the pathways that Jesus has spoken over our lives. It will not be fulfilled unless and until it finds its home in Jesus, in whom every promise of God finds its "Yes!" (see 2 Corinthians 1:20).

God's promises call us forward out of the shadows of death. ("Moses my servant is dead.") The bluntness and the brevity of this statement must have been both devastating and liberating. Without God's promises it will be easy for us to languish in death—grief, disappointments, shame, failure, missed expectations. This is not the "kingdom" the child of God is called to inhabit.

God's promises are linked to our personal histories. ("As I was with Moses . . .") God's promises may destine us toward something heretofore unimagined but they do not disregard those life experiences that God has authored to shape us and make us ready for His call.

God's promises have continuity with God's character and other promises. ("As I promised Moses . . .") We need not fear that the pursuit of God's promises are going to set us up for some kind of bizarre mystical experience. God's promises are not new revelations. They are particular application of the promises of God, already fulfilled in Christ, for you. Twice in this passage God reiterates that this promise is consistent with what He has previously promised.

God's promises declare God's high purposes for us. ("Now . . . cross the Jordan . . .") I can only say that God's kingdom purposes for you are higher and more strategic than you can imagine on your own. From His perspective you have a Jordan to cross, a land to possess and a tomorrow to walk into.

Until next week . . .

Confident in the Person of Jesus

His name will be called Wonderful (Isaiah 9:6)

There are 256 names given in the Bible for our Lord Jesus Christ. I imagine this is because He is infinitely beyond all that any one name can express.[1]

Isaiah prophesied that Jesus shall be called Wonderful. Wonderful describes:

Someone who is transcendently beyond the common . . .
Someone who exceeds the ordinary . . .
Someone who serendipitously stirs the soul with astonishment . . .
Someone who ineffably woos the heart, engages the mind, and ennobles the spirit . . .

Is Jesus Wonderful? Consider His birth—no other has ever occurred like it. He could have come amidst pomp and ceremony or He could have been born in a palace and rocked in a golden cradle while attended by angels. But even this would have been a great condescension for Him. Instead Jesus comes incognito, yet not anonymously. The swaddling clothes wrap the Baby whose flesh wraps the glory which is His incarnation. His name shall be called Wonderful . . .

Is Jesus Wonderful? Consider His character—no one else has ever approached its perfection. He is sinless but never self-righteous. Rich and poor, male and female, Jew and Gentile, legalist and hedonist, prostitute and Pharisee are equally welcomed by Him. His love is relentless, His favor is unbiased and His example is unmatched. After living closely with Jesus for three years His closest friends esteem Him so highly that they worship Him as Messiah, Lord and Savior. His name shall be called Wonderful . . .

Is Jesus Wonderful? Consider His life—no other has ever lived as Jesus lived. He came to bless and not to curse; to lift up and not to cast down; to save and not to destroy; to free and not to oppress. There has never been the slightest hint of selfishness or self-interest found in the testimonies of His life. He never used His authority or His power for personal gain. He had the power to turn stones into bread and yet went without food for forty days. He fed crowds, wept for cities, healed the sick, ignored barriers of gender and race, blessed His enemies, forgave His killers and purposely gave His life as a ransom for sin. His name shall be called Wonderful . . .

Is Jesus Wonderful? Consider His teaching—no other has taught what Jesus taught. His teaching is simple and clear but never patronizing or condescending. He is original and never pedantic. His parables reflect His creativity and His exhortations manifest His authority. He came without credentials and made claims that are humanly unbelievable. He wrote no sermons, dictated no letters, published no books, founded no school and committed His message to uneducated fishermen. Yet His teaching has endured for 2,000 years and has lifted nations and peoples out of darkness and degradation. His name shall be called Wonderful . . .

Is Jesus Wonderful? Consider this: When Jesus was born, Rome ruled the world. Her invincible power and ubiquitous influence secured her an empire without rival in world history. Thirty-three years later, in one of her least esteemed provinces, a Man was crucified for sedition according to Roman law. His execution would have gone unnoticed by 99.99 percent of the empire. This Man never launched an army nor did He ever carry a sword. On no occasion did He ever incite violence or organize a revolution. He exhorted His followers to pay their taxes, healed a centurion's servant and taught His followers to bless their persecutors. Humanly speaking, His teaching should have been completely forgotten within a generation. Neither Rome or Israel embraced it as mainstream or practical.

Within 300 years of His death the teaching of Jesus dominated Rome. By then His life and teachings had been carried further than the empire had ever reached. Today Rome is a capital but not an empire. Her power is gone, her temples lie in ruins and her gods forgotten.

Today more people call on the name of Jesus than any other name. He has overcome every barrier known to humanity—gender, class, nation, culture, race, tongue and *time*. Oriental and occidental are within His grasp. Two thousand years later the world continues to be shaken by the compelling and relevant testimony of Jesus. You have only to lift up your head and look about you to see the wonder of His presence impacting our world today. His name shall be called Wonderful. . . . Is Jesus Wonderful? Oh, yes! He is wonderful and so much more.

He is Counselor . . .
  He is Mighty . . .
    He is God . . .
      He is Everlasting . . .
    He is Father . . .
  He is Prince of Peace . . .
Of the increase of His government and peace there will be no end . . .

Until next week . . .

Confident in Our Coming King

Now there was a man in Jerusalem called Simeon, who was righteous and devout. He was waiting for the consolation of Israel, and the Holy Spirit was upon him. It had been revealed to him by the Holy Spirit that he would not die before he had seen the Lord's Christ. Moved by the Spirit, he went into the temple courts. When the parents brought in the child Jesus to do for him what the custom of the Law required, Simeon took him in his arms and praised God, saying:

> "Sovereign Lord, as you have promised,
>   you now dismiss your servant in
>   peace.
> For my eyes have seen your salvation,
>   which you have prepared in the sight
>   of all people,
> a light for revelation to the Gentiles
>   and for glory to your people Israel."

(Luke 2:25-32, NIV)

His heart was beating fast; quickened by an awakening of the Holy Spirit that echoed back to an earlier day . . . an earlier promise that was seared into his soul by God: "Simeon, you will not see the darkness of your death until you see the Light of the world. Look and keep looking! Behold, He is coming . . ."

The whole world changed for Simeon that day . . .

All things final
   now looked temporary . . .
Everything substantial
   now seemed as a shadow of things to come . . .
The grip of tyranny
   now appeared to be slipping . . .
The monopoly of sin, death and demonic evil
   now appeared usurped . . .
The promises of God, once distant,
   now pressed in upon his soul
     with imminent urgency.

The world changed for Simeon that day . . .

Now, each new dawn might be the world's last . . .
   Every man's face might be *His* face . . .
Any incident might be a sign for His coming . . .
   Simeon was now a seeker . . .
     his nights would be
       an occasion for disappointment
        if he did not behold Him, and
his mornings an opportunity for new hope—
     this could be the day!

The world changed for Simeon that day . . . and his daily, hourly and minute-by-minute challenge would be that his world would not change back to what it was before . . . a life without expectation.

And so it was that his aging heart was beating fast as he scanned the temple courts for a man of stature . . . a commanding presence . . . a self-authenticating bearing and authority that betrayed a Messianic identity. Instead his soul leapt within him when his gaze fell upon a nondescript couple that cradled a six-week-old Child in their arms. Unbelievably, it was not the father but the Baby who commanded his attention. He took the Child into his arms and looked through the veil of His flesh *into the face of God*:

> "For my eyes have seen your salvation,
>   which you have prepared in the sight
>   of all people,
> a light for revelation to the Gentiles
>   and for glory to your people Israel."
>
> (Luke 2:30-32, NIV)

My heart is quickened by the opportunity to look into the face of the Child Messiah as the Holy Spirit challenges me to confess aloud what I see:

I see in Jesus the Promised One of God who is

the Son of Abraham
    in whom all nations on earth can be blessed;

the Son of David
  who establishes and reigns over a kingdom
    that has no end;
the Messiah
  who comes to deliver His people from
    bondage;
the Suffering Servant
  who bears the punishment my sins deserve;
the Son of Man
  who came to serve and give
    His life as a ransom for many.

I see in Jesus the Lamb of God
who makes atonement and takes away
  the sin of the world;
who overcomes the reproach of my sin;
who covers over my shame;
who forgives me of my guilt;
who reconciles me to God and others.

I see in Jesus the Son of God
  the Creator who has become a Creature;
  the One in whom all things hold together;
  the One by whom and for whom
    I was made;
the One whose face
  is the face of the invisible God;
the One who exemplifies
  all we were meant to be; and
the One who is like
  what we, by His grace, shall be.

I see in Jesus the Love of God
   that reaches out to the outcast;
   that invites the overlooked;
   that befriends without prejudice;
   that satisfies the hungry
     and satiates the thirsty;
   that will never leave, forsake
     or abandon me.

I see in Jesus the Power of God
   that stills the wind and calms the waves;
   that heals the sick;
   that breaks the strongholds of evil;
   that delivers the afflicted;
   that liberates the oppressed and harassed;
   that baptizes us with the Holy Spirit.

I see in Jesus the Blessed Hope of God.
   When He returns it will be
     the end of death, decay and evil;
the finish of injustice, corruption,
     prejudice and greed;
the termination of sin's despair,
     depravity and defilement;
the close of insignificance, estrangement,
     abandonment and futility;
the end of *now* and the beginning of forever;
the fulfillment of our unfulfillment;
the final joy in whom I shall take pleasure.

I see in Jesus
   the Once and Future Lamb of God
who will wipe every tear from the mourning;

who will overcome every advocacy of evil;
who will vanquish the ravages of sin;
who covers all shame
  with the robes of His righteousness;
who will welcome the poor and broken;
who will light all eternity
  and dispel night forever.

I see in Jesus our Coming King:
  Resplendent is His majesty;
    Triumphant is His victory;
Magnificent is His authority;
  Jubilant is His shout;
Death-defeating is His roar;
  "It is done" will be His song!

I confess along with Martin Luther, "I have no other God than the one who once rested on Mary's lap."

Loved ones, who do you see as you look into the face of the baby Jesus? Is He your blessed hope? Do you have assurance that He can be your consolation too? If you are uncertain, why not take a moment to pray,

"Jesus, come into my life and be my blessed hope and consolation."

With expectation for the Coming King . . .

PART TWO:

Purposeful

It is the absence of purpose that breeds failure and aimlessness not the absence of talent. Do not be content to creep when God has purposed you to soar.

God Is Purposeful

The Son of God appeared for this purpose, to destroy the works of the devil. (1 John 3:8)

God is purposeful . . .
  No exercise of His might,
    no declaration of His wisdom,
      and no expression of His love
        is trivial, capricious or random.

God is purposeful . . .
He does not say one thing and do another.
  He does not undermine His own advance
    through indecision or retraction.
      He does not take three steps forward
        and two steps back.

God is purposeful . . .
He is undeterred, unhindered and undistracted.
  His love is resolute and
    His tenderness is relentless.
      Therefore He will never turn away
        until He has accomplished everything
      that He has purposed
    within the counsel of His will.

God is purposeful . . .
In Jesus dwelled the fullness of God
  and the fullness of God's purpose.
In Jesus God purposed to become man
  in order to take up our case.
In Jesus God closes the breach, gulf and abyss
  between God and us, for which
  we are responsible.

God is purposeful . . .
At the very point where we
  refuse and fail
    offend and provoke
      miss our destiny
        tread underfoot our dignity,
          and lose our salvation,
  God purposed to intervene as a man
    in the person and work of Jesus.

God is purposeful . . .
He makes no mistakes.
  He has no regrets.
    He faces our future with
      unrestricted liberty
      uncompromising devotion
      unlimited resources
      unbounded wisdom
      and unconditional love.

God is purposeful . . .
Before your parents conceived you,
  He conceived you.
You are not an accident,

nor are you the fruit of a moment's passion.
You were deliberately fashioned
  and richly endowed.
You were born of God's purpose
  and you were born for God's purpose.

God is purposeful . . .
Therefore, I urge you to recite and prayerfully reflect on the following five statements as we begin to explore God's strategic purpose for your life.

1. I have a purpose.
2. My purpose is to transform lives with the person and power of Jesus Christ.
3. I will not be satisfied with my life until I am fulfilling my purpose.
4. I can best fulfill my purpose as part of a team.
5. I have no promise of mortal life tomorrow—therefore, I must fulfill my purpose today![2]

Until next week . . .

You Have a Purpose

God is purposeful . . .
Before your parents conceived you
   He conceived you.
You are not an accident,
   nor are you the fruit of a moment's passion.
You were deliberately fashioned
   and richly endowed.
You were born of God's purpose
   and you were born for God's purpose.

have a purpose. Everyone who has been twice born through Jesus Christ has been lovingly and strategically created for a purpose. There is nothing more tragic than aimless Christians who have lost their grasp of this simple reality. Purposelessness is surely a barometric reading on the true condition of our soul. The plethora of self-help titles in Christian bookstores suggests that we have exchanged the great ends of the Church for the trifling illusion that personal fulfillment is merely reflected in emotional well-being and daily convenience. This is narcissism, not discipleship.

God's purpose for us, and through us, is robust, life-affirming and fruitful. It will add dimension and meaning to every facet of our lives and will endow every relationship, every opportunity and all our time with significance.

My purpose is to impact people with the person and power of Jesus Christ. Spiritual warfare is not an option for the follower of Jesus Christ. Evil is real. The devil will not go away unless he is put to flight. The Scriptures testify that Jesus came to destroy the works of the evil one. This is our purpose too.

I concede that it is difficult to look in the mirror and recite, "My purpose is to destroy the works of the evil one." I know because I tried it on several occasions and felt foolish! I found that the moment I declared aloud, "My purpose is to destroy the works of the evil one," I was defeated by thoughts of my own powerlessness. (Not even my dog comes when I call!)

I was liberated when the Holy Spirit led me to a study of First John 3:8. I discovered that the Greek word translated "destroy" is more frequently translated "loose" or "untie" in the New Testament. There I remembered one of my favorite sweaters being destroyed by my oldest daughter when she was three. She merely found a dangling strand that she continued to pull until an entire sleeve was gone! Every day I meet people bound with the devil's dangling strands—that I can pull with the person and power of Jesus Christ.

I will not be satisfied with my life until I am fulfilling my purpose. You are created and called by God for a purpose. Embedded deep within you are yearnings whose origins lie in the eternal heart of God. Living for the trophies of this world will never satiate these longings. Their home is the kingdom of God. Seek first the kingdom of God and you will gain the personal satisfaction you long for.

I can best fulfill my purpose as part of a team. We cannot fulfill our purpose alone. The most talented basketball or baseball player will never win a game unless he participates on a team. There is nothing Satan appreciates more than unplugged Christians who are adrift from the body of Christ, distracted by the world's allure and preoccupied with their own happiness.

I have no promise of mortal life tomorrow, even though I have the promise of eternal life forever. We have no way of knowing when illness, accident or violence may end our mortal lives. Live the life you are called to today. Look around you—your life is full of opportunities to untie and loose the works of the devil in the lives of others. Go on . . . pull those strings . . .

Until next week . . .

You Have a Purpose for Such a Time as This . . .

The Son of God appeared for this purpose, to destroy the works of the devil. (1 John 3:8)

Who knows whether you have not attained royalty for such a time as this? (Esther 4:14)

God is purposeful . . .
Therefore I have a purpose . . .
My purpose is to impact people
    with the person and power of Jesus Christ.
I will not be satisfied with my life
    until I am fulfilling my purpose.
I can best fulfill my purpose as part of a team.
I have no promise of mortal life tomorrow . . .

Please indulge me as I tell you a true story. It was a golden age: The nation had triumphed at war; the economy was prosperous; the people enjoyed their newfound affluence. The nation enjoyed her emerging status as a world superpower. Women of wealth enjoyed elaborate cosmetic makeovers (a combination of diet, exercise and beauty treatments) while other notable women contested for respect and their rights. Nevertheless, it was still a conservative era when every man was encouraged to be king of his own castle.

The country is Persia. The place is Susa, the nation's capital. The time is 486-465 B.C. The king is Ahasuerus, in the third year of his reign, and his queen is Esther. Her ascent to the throne came by way of her beauty, not her bloodline. She was truly the Cinderella—the Lady Diana—of her day. Her life as a royal was a far cry from the life she had known as a child.

Esther, born Hadassah, was orphaned when her parents were taken captive in Jerusalem and carried away to Persia. She was adopted and raised by her older cousin, Mordecai, under whose tutelage was imparted a love for her Jewish heritage and faith. And so it was that Hadassah, the spoil of war, became the young woman Esther—a woman whose beauty and grace would ultimately capture the king's gaze and later his affection. Twelve months after their first meeting she would be made queen. By all accounts she was loved and popular; her husband even established a national holiday in her honor. But there is a storm on the horizon and Esther is on a collision course with her destiny. . . .

Ahasuerus appoints a new prime minister who conspires to settle the Jewish question once and for all. He capitalizes upon the pride and prejudice of his day as he promises the king a great multiplication of wealth once the Jews are disposed of. (Some arguments never change. Genocide is now the order of the day.)

Mordecai enjoins Esther to use her position of influence to stay the king's hand, but he is abruptly rebuffed. Esther professes helplessness and protests that she too will be killed if she walks into the king's inner court uninvited. But Mordecai will not be dissuaded and exhorts her with words that ring out across the centuries: "And who knows whether you have not attained royalty for such a time as this?" (Esther 4:14).

🕭 🕭 🕭 🕭 🕭

The book of Esther exhorts us to rediscover our sense of purpose. Like Esther, it is not by accident that you are where you are. Even if this is a season of transition, you have a God-given purpose for being where you are. If not you, then who is God calling to exercise the watchful care of others where you are? If not you, then who is God calling to show forth energy, fidelity, tenacity, generosity and grace where you are? If not you, then who is God calling to serve sacrificially and illumine the presence of Jesus and His kingdom where you are? If not you, then who? Who knows? Perhaps you are where you are for such a time as this. . . .

Until next week . . .

Discover Your Purpose . . .

And who knows whether you have not attained royalty for such a time as this? (Esther 4:14)

Our culture looks toward the future with a curious blend of anticipation, anxiety and antipathy. Some predict years of unparalleled economic growth and international cooperation while others see devastation brought on by environmental decay and militant nationalism. Others just see the "same ol' same ol'." One thing is certain: This millennial "shadow" provides followers of Jesus Christ with an opportune moment to influence and lead our world. To say it another way: "Behold, I say to you, lift up your eyes and look on the fields, that they are white for harvest" (John 4:35). It is no accident that you are alive for such a time as this.

God is purposeful. . . .

Before your parents conceived you,
    He conceived you.

You are not an accident,
> nor are you the fruit of a moment's passion.

You were deliberately fashioned
> and richly endowed.

You were born of God's purpose
> and you were born for God's purpose.

Therefore anyone who recognizes that they have been created by God and born twice through Jesus Christ can confidently say:

I have a purpose. . . .
My purpose is to transform lives
> with the person and power of Jesus Christ.

I will not be satisfied with my life
> until I am fulfilling my purpose.

I can best fulfill my purpose as part of a team.
I have no promise of mortal life tomorrow. . . .

How do we (re)discover our sense of purpose? Let me suggest four simple affirmations:

1. ***Acknowledge*** *that your purpose exists even if you do not know what it is!* Consider your gifts and your inclinations . . . significant life experiences (both the good and the bad) . . . those toward whom you have compassion . . . strategic answers to your prayers . . . biblical promises/ verses that have always stayed with you . . . life-shaping Christian experiences . . . your present circumstances . . . your spiritual gifts . . . your primary relationships . . . your core values.

2. ***Admit*** *that you cannot (re)discover your purpose without God.* While your sense of purpose

may be galvanized through reflection, reading and relationships, it will not be catalyzed apart from God's inspiration. There is a world of difference between being called and being driven. Good intentions are no substitute for strategic living. "Think of yourself with sober judgment, in accordance with the measure of faith God has given you" (Romans 12:3, NIV).

3. ***Accept*** *the place of your purpose even if you are uncertain where it ultimately is!* When I go shopping with my oldest daughter, she is certain that the perfect outfit for her is somewhere in the mall even if she doesn't know where it is when we start out! (I can only guarantee you that it will never be in the first couple of stores we visit!) Do not underestimate the value of the search itself. Your present circumstances, relationships, opportunities, the Scriptures you read and the prayers you pray are essential milestones along the way. They reveal, refine and redirect us as we seek to be embraced by God's purpose in our lives.

4. ***Assent*** *that whatever your purpose, it is good in the eyes of God.* Do not let ego obscure or mar the significance of God's purpose through you. We must be ready to surrender the stage of human favor for the prayer closet of our Father's pleasure. This week take ten minutes to read the book of Ruth—the most faithful daughter-in-law who ever lived! Her purpose in life was to live faithfully—nothing more and noth-

ing less. But her purposeful living was a strategic link in the chain of God's redemptive
purpose. Ruth was the great-grandmother of
King David and given the right to be an ances-
tor, in the human lineage, of Jesus.

You were born of God's purpose and you were
born for God's purpose. Pray about this in the
days ahead.

Until next week . . .

PART THREE

Devoted

Any relationship that lacks devotion is little more than an acquaintance. Devotion is the barometric reading of God's grace in the life of His beloved.

Devoted to Worship (Part 1)

Through Jesus, therefore, let us continually offer to God a sacrifice of praise—the fruit of lips that confess his name. And do not forget to do good and to share with others, for with such sacrifices God is pleased. (Hebrews 13:15-16, NIV)

Worship is the:

- ❦ first great commandment (Exodus 20:1-8; Luke 10:27).
- ❦ first action we should take when we come into God's presence—"Enter His gates with thanksgiving!" (see Psalms 30 and 100).
- ❦ first response we should make when we come to faith in Jesus Christ (1 Peter 2:4-5).
- ❦ first mark of the Holy Spirit in our lives (Galatians 4:29).
- ❦ first sign of the Holy Spirit at Pentecost (Acts 2).
- ❦ first priority of the early Church (Acts 2:46-47).

- ❦ first reaction we should have when in trouble (Acts 4:24-26).
- ❦ first thing we should do in prayer (see Matthew 6:9).
- ❦ first expression of those who desire to hear God (Luke 1:5-25; Acts 10:9; 13:1).
- ❦ first and ceaseless language of heaven (Revelation 4:8; 5:14).

God is looking for people who are worshipers first rather than people who are workers. Most people, however, value work more than they value worship. This is not only backward in God's sight, it is also dangerous to the Christian life, because it is human destiny to either serve a lie or to serve the Truth.

Every man possesses a shrine somewhere . . .
   in his heart . . .
      in his mind . . .
         in his life . . . or
            in the essence of his being
in which there is a "deity" whom he serves with
   his strength,
      ingenuity,
         imagination,
            emotion,
               ability
                  and time.
This god my be
   yourself . . .
      your spouse . . .
         your children . . .

　　　　your esteem . . .
　　　　　　your comfort . . .
　　　　　　　　your career . . .
　　　　　　your ministry . . .
　　　　your cause . . .
　　your church . . .
　your aspirations . . . or
your love for money, sexual gratification
and/or power.

Everything I have seen tells me that it is as impossible for someone to live without having an object of devotion as it is for an eagle to refrain from flight. The very composition of human life, the mystery of man's being and our inherent ambition and yearning all demand a center of worship that is necessary for a fulfilling and purposeful existence. The question is whether your life and powers will be devoted in worship to the *true* God or to a *false* one. Do not be deceived. *Your life is a transparent testimony of who or what you worship.* Christian pretense and jargon cannot conceal to those around us who or what we value most.

Until next week . . .

Devoted to Worship (Part 2)

*By faith Abel offered God a better
sacrifice than Cain did. By faith he was
commended as a righteous man, when
God spoke well of his offerings. And by
faith he still speaks, even though he is
dead. (Hebrews 11:4, NIV)*

Baseball fans must travel to Cooperstown, New York to visit the Baseball Hall of Fame. However, you will not have to travel to Israel to visit the Bible's Old Testament Hall of Fame. You will find it located in Hebrews 11. There you will revisit the exploits of Abraham, Sarah, Noah, Isaac, Jacob, Joseph, Moses, Joshua, Rehab, Gideon, Samson, David, Samuel and Abel.

At first sight, Abel is a curious choice for entry into this hall of fame. He is mentioned in only three Old Testament verses and he is the victim of the first murder recorded in Scripture. His name means "vanity" or "mere breath." He led no armies, wrote no books, left no wisdom and had no disciples. He is a "nobody" when compared to the giants of Scripture—but then God delights to make nobodies into "somebodies" in His sight where there is even a kernel of authentic faith.

There are three important things to notice about Abel. *First, by faith he worshiped: He "offered God . . . a sacrifice."* Worship is more important than work, ministry, family or our witness for Christ. Workers can devote themselves to their labor for numerous reasons—money, success, power, prestige, influence, love or pleasing others—yet rarely is worship at the top of their motivational list. A worshiper works to exalt God—his labors are a response to God's call. People sometimes say, "I went to such-and-such a church but I didn't get anything out of it." The question is, "What did you put into it?" First we worship, then we receive; that's the proper order of things in the kingdom of God.

Second, by faith Abel was accepted by God: "God spoke well of his offerings." The story of Cain and Abel's sacrifices (Genesis 4:3-5) seems unfair at first sight. Yet if we study this passage in its context we soon realize that God had previously shown Cain and Abel what offerings would be acceptable to Him. Faith's "hall of fame" in Hebrews 11 is comprised of men and women who, by faith, obeyed God's word to them. So it must have been that Abel, by faith, obeyed while Cain gave the sacrifice he deemed adequate and good enough.

Some people struggle in their walk with God because they don't feel accepted by Him. But perhaps it is because what we offer Him through our worship is unacceptable. God will forgive sin and He will save sinners. God will *not* accept pretense, rationalized sin and halfhearted devotion even when it is offered, as Cain did, as an act of worship. Can God really accept just two percent when He has called us to worship with ten percent? Can He accept compromise when He has called us to integrity? Will God accept our double-minded lust when He has called us to single-minded purity? This is not an issue of grace by faith alone; it is an issue of carelessness and thoughtlessness masquerading as worship. Worship is not a "bone" we throw to satisfy God. King David understood it well when he exclaimed, "I will not offer burnt offerings to the LORD my God which cost me nothing" (2 Samuel 24:24).

Third, by faith Abel still speaks. Whatever is done by faith, in obedience to God's Word, has the stamp of eternity on it. TV shows, books, articles, etc., deluge us with talk of retirement and estate planning. Our ultimate goal in life is to leave a legacy of faith that will speak to the generations that follow us. They may not remember our name, as we do Abel's, but God promises that our faithfulness will preach to the generations to come. Our race will not be in vain.

Until next week . . .

Devoted to Prayer (Part 1)

When they heard this, they raised their voices together in prayer to God. (Acts 4:24, NIV)

Prayer is a powerful word. Mention it in a room full of Christians and watch the tone of the conversation become subdued. Invite people to dinner and faces light up. Invite someone to a time to pray together and anxiety arises. Most participants in churches across the country will find something else that demands their time rather than attend a prayer gathering—even when the gathering is scheduled on a night and time when a previously attended weekly event occurs! Most followers of Jesus Christ say they should pray more, but most of us rarely do. We can recite pat quips that "prayer is the most powerful thing we can do" but other less "powerful" pursuits generally seem to crowd it out. Nationwide, the average attendance at prayer meetings is running between ten and twenty percent of a congregation's attendance. How can something that God intended as a gift foster so much intimidation and remorse? Is it possible that we have created an expectation for prayer that very few individuals can live up to?

In the Western world we see prayer as the secluded exercise of the individual who wishes to converse with God. Our thinking on this has been shaped by frequent references to Jesus' criticism of the Pharisees, who used public prayer for their own self-aggrandizement (see Matthew 6:5-8). However, when we turn to Scripture we see quite a different picture emerge. Here we discover hundreds of examples of people praying together. In fact there are far more references to people praying together than we have references to praying alone. I am not suggesting that we abandon private prayer. I am asking whether we are expecting from private prayer what only corporate prayer can provide. Could it be that we need the complete body of Christ to have a rich, meaningful and effective prayer life?

In other parts of the world the emphasis is not on private prayer but corporate prayer gatherings. Nations that have seen God's hand manifest in remarkable ways are nations whose Christian population have made a deliberate effort to come together to intercede on behalf of their city, region, nation and world. In these countries the weekly all-church prayer gathering is a fixture in congregational life. In these nations the number of churches gathering each week to pray are on the rise. In these countries church growth is on the rise rather than at an eleven-year low as in the United States.

In the United States many bemoan our nation's loss of spirituality, character and morality. Some have even shown a correlation between the prohibition on prayer in public school and our nation's cultural decline. I would wager that these public restrictions on prayer directly reflect the Church's neglect of her own corporate prayer life. Weekly prayer gatherings are commonly seen as unnecessary, a throwback to an unsophisticated Christian worldview, the preoccupation of fanatics, an unrealistic expectation for those who are already too busy and/or an elective opportunity for "those" kind of people. Why should we expect schools to emphasize what the Church will not?

Why are we so impassioned about school prayer when the Church in America will not gather to pray together as she once did? The First Great Awakening, The Second Great Awakening, the abolition and missionary movements of the latter eighteenth century, and the New York Revival at the turn of the century are just a mere sampling of historic movements of God that have been punctuated by weekly prayer gatherings. Regular corporate prayer gatherings cannot force God's hand to do anything that He has not determined in the counsel of His loving will. That God has chosen to use corporate prayer to accomplish His purposes is a fact. This begs the question of frequency—must it be weekly? I would simply suggest something between zero and weekly would be a good place to start!

Until next week . . .

Devoted to Prayer (Part 2)

There are many recipes for the destruction of a nation. Yet each shares a single ingredient—the repudiation of the uniqueness, authority, supremacy and clarity of God's revelation through the Scriptures. The results are the same whether this repudiation is obscured by passive indifference or blatantly promoted. The outright rejection of His Word has produced a cornucopia of wickedness that is destroying this nation from the inside out.

Now I readily admit that "wickedness" is a strong word. It assaults the sensibilities of modern, tolerance. Nevertheless it is a word that we would be well advised to rediscover. The Bible speaks of wickedness when individual sin becomes embedded in the national or cultural psyche and influences the practices of a people or nation. Thus a person in ancient Israel may, for example, sin through the worship of other gods, but the nation becomes wicked only when it tolerates and promulgates the same practice on a national level.

Again, there is an individual sin of lust and adultery, but it becomes a matter of wickedness when that same practice is encouraged or tolerated nationwide.

The peril of wickedness is real because its nature is to maim, plunder and destroy. It does not esteem the rich more highly than the poor. It does not favor one gender or ethnic group above another. It does not defer to the innocence of childhood or the wisdom of the mature. It does not distinguish between urban, residential or rural. Wickedness destroys.

Wickedness is not a "contagion" that you can quarantine. Nor does it simply expire after it has run its course. There are only two ways to defeat it: Destroy it and the people it has infected, or overcome it through the life, death and resurrection of Jesus Christ. This is the living hope that the Church—the people of God—is called to present boldly in the midst of a crooked and perverse generation, among whom we appear as lights in the world, holding fast the word of life (Philippians 2:15).

Many are the recipes humanity has concocted for the destruction of a nation. God offers us one for its healing:

> If my people, who are called by my name,
> will humble themselves and pray and seek
> my face and turn from their wicked ways,
> then will I hear from heaven and will for-

give their sin and will heal their land. (2 Chronicles 7:14, NIV)

This passage reminds us of a simple truth we would prefer to forget: God's plan for any nation begins with the people who bear His name. Therefore . . .

We must humble ourselves. We must confess that we have not been singular in our devotion to God. While we are rich in silver and gold, we lack the power of God that is released through humility. We hide our hesitancy to share the gospel of Jesus Christ behind such labels as "tactful," "considerate" and "tolerant." We walk with Christ as peers rather than following Him in reverent submission as His disciples. We are dismayed each time our cultural institutions eschew public prayer, yet the average church in America no longer has prayer meetings. We are outraged each time the courts deny the posting of Scripture in public places, and yet the average Christian posts no Scripture in the marketplace. These are not the issues of the Christian Right. These are the fundamental issues of Christian righteousness. We must relearn the heart cry of biblical humility: "Yet not my will but Yours, O God."

We must pray and seek God's face. Consistent and focused prayer that will persist despite time and circumstances—this is the kind of prayer that creates strategic witness and ministry, changes lives, subverts governments and influences nations. The relationship between the du-

ration of prayer and the answers to prayer is a
mystery that cannot be systematized. Yet it is the
witness of Scripture and reiterated by experience
that the prayer that releases salvation and deliv-
erance will certainly exceed the attention spans
of any generation that lives for personal convenience and instant gratification.

We must turn from our wicked ways. We, the
Church, are hamstrung by the very sins that jeop-
ardize this nation: idolatry, an indifference to
worship, a withholding of our tithes and offerings, greed, racism, a neglect of the poor, abor-
tion, divorce, addiction, pornography, a partisan
spirit and enslavement to debt. It is hard to ex-
emplify the pursuit of God when we are entan-
gled by the very same wickedness that has
overcome the world.

It is time for us to invite the Spirit of God to convict us of this simple truth: How different our lives
and world will be once the household of God turns
afresh toward our beautiful Savior with contrition
and in humility. Enough is enough! Let us draw
near for cleansing and renewal.

Until next week . . .

Devoted to Prayer (Part 3)

. . . you also joining in helping us through your prayers. . . . For though we walk in the flesh, we do not war according to the flesh, for the weapons of our warfare are not of the flesh, but divinely powerful for the destruction of fortresses. (2 Corinthians 1:11; 10:3-4)

Of all the Christians I know who take their faith seriously, I do not know a single one who does not want his whole life to count for Christ. Each of us wants to be used by God to influence people and impact our world. We want to participate in the eternal legacy of Jesus Christ. We who have been magnetized and empowered by His love naturally want to magnetize and empower others. Let me suggest one method that is tried and true—it has changed individuals, transformed whole families, demolished walls of racism and ethnic strife and even toppled civilizations. I shall call it the "stealth" method—you know it more simply as prayer.

There is a fascinating verse in Paul's second letter to the Corinthians where he invites their prayerful support for his evangelistic work. In verse 11 of the first chapter he literally says: "You also helping together underneath in prayer." What could such a phrase mean to Paul?[3]

I believe that he is thinking of the fortresses and walled cities that were such common structures in the ancient world. Evangelism involves storming strongholds like that in people's lives. But a frontal assault is often useless. What is needed is a tunnel. This will require hard work, sustained work and teamwork. Such effort is unseen and unsung, but it is crucial if the fortress is to be taken. Prayer is like that. It assails the inner recesses of a man's will in a way that all our talking cannot.

J.I. Packer writes,

> However clear and cogent we may be in our presentation of the gospel, we have no hope of convincing and converting anyone. Can you or I by earnest talking break the power of Satan over a man's life? No! Can you or I give life to the spiritually dead? No! Can we hope to convince sinners of the truth of the gospel by patent explanation? No! Can we hope to move men to believe the gospel by any words of entreaty that we may utter? No! Our approach to evangelism is not realistic until we have faced this

shattering fact, and let it make its proper impact upon us.[4]

Now let me confess to you at once that all of this is counterintuitive for me. By temperament I would much rather storm walls than "tunnel away" in prayer. But time and experience continue to confront me with the reality that it is the tunneling which counts and prevails.

Foolish is the Christian—and I have been just such a fool—who does not remember that reality exceeds the yardstick of the scientist. There are natural laws for the realities of nature, and there spiritual laws which are natural to the realities of the kingdom of God. In the natural realms gravity can exert a force which causes things to fall. In spiritual realms prayer can exert a force that, while unseen in the natural, has the capacity to cause "things" to fall.

The fall of Jericho (Joshua 6) testifies to the power of God's ways. God instructed the Israelites to march around Jericho for six days in a huge worship procession. Then on the seventh day they marched again, gave a shout unto the Lord and the city walls collapsed. Israel's victory was not the fruit of their prodigious vocal strength! Victory came because something "subterranean" was happening in the spiritual realm that would breach the structural integrity of the walls in the natural realm.

The movement of God always begins in "spiritual places." The call to Abraham, the Exodus, the selection of David, the prophets' vision, the coming of Jesus, the day of Pentecost—from where did these come? From the realms of nature or the realm of the Spirit? Prayer is the one tool that God has given us to impact the wicked spiritual realm which buttresses the bastions of evil, sin and brokenness in and around us.

So if you feel like you are banging your head against a wall that will not budge, perhaps it is time to start tunneling.

Until next week . . .

Devoted to God's Word

Now the Bereans were of more noble character than the Thessalonians, for they received the message with great eagerness and examined the Scriptures every day to see if what Paul said was true. (Acts 17:11-12, NIV)

The message they heard was of no value to them, because those who heard did not combine it with faith. (Hebrews 4:2, NIV)

The Bible is still the world's best-selling book. Here in North America publishers rush to commission new translations or package the Scriptures in different editions. I recently counted fourteen versions of the same translation in a local bookstore, including editions specifically for men, women, senior citizens, African-Americans, children and youth. In addition, this same translation offered the Classical Devotional Bible, the Chronological Bible and the Quiet

Time Bible, along with editions representing every interest under the sun—historical/textual understanding, endtimes/prophecy, charismatic, dispensational, praise and worship, and topical/thematic. Best-selling authors have even produced editions with their own devotional notations.

Yet despite its prolific distribution, most people who participate in a local church cannot recite the Ten Commandments (in any order), feel inadequate to study the Scriptures on their own and spend less than ten minutes each week (including Sunday) in Bible reading. Few have any kind of disciplined study time. When asked, "Why do you think the Bible is important?" the common response is, "It is a spiritual book."

The Bible *is* a spiritual book. Its many writers, spanning at least 1,600 years, were inspired by the Spirit of God to give us His Word—a word for all people everywhere and for all time. It is a spiritual book, but it is not a magical book. Scripture is not a good luck talisman that secures good fortune by virtue of its possession. Biblical possession is not nine-tenths of the law—receptivity and responsiveness are! Because the Bible is a spiritual book, we need the Holy Spirit to help us understand it. However, we also have a part to play—and the people of Berea set us a good example here.

First, they were willing to learn; they received the message. Before we read the Bible, we need to be quiet in God's presence and ask Him to speak to us. Microsoft's® ad campaign for their software products asks the right question: "Where do you want to go today?" The question implies movement and destination. Followers of Jesus Christ will start their day asking the same question with the addition of one little word: "Where do You want *me* to go today?"

Second, they were disciplined; they examined the Scriptures every day. This is where Bible study and reading notes can be so helpful. According to your age, ability and appetite, there are notes and commentaries that can guide you through the entire Bible, through a particular book or through a section of Scripture.

Third, they were obedient; many of them believed and acted on God's Word. The Scriptures are not for those who are merely curious or desirous of more knowledge. It is a book that is written to change lives. It provokes a response; it expects action.

The danger in many biblically based churches is that we become congregations who enjoy "message-tasting." Message-tasters are those who like to sample the truth and authority of Scripture, yet rarely read it, study it, submit to it or act on it. Message-tasting abounds on Sunday morning when most gather to worship and hear the Scriptures and a message. Messages are then subjected to a "spiritual palate" which has some similarities with its cousin, "wine-tasting." This palate includes color (did it make me feel good?), consistency (is it consistent with what I like to hear?) and content (was it interesting to me?).

Several years ago a self-confessing Christian from the congregation I serve as pastor said to me, "I am going to leave your church because your sermons don't do anything for me."

We talked for a while and then I asked two questions: "Do you read the Bible regularly during the week? Do you take time to pray and ask God to speak to you and teach you His truth during the week?" The answer to both questions was, "No, not really." I concluded our conversation by observing, "How do you expect my words to have any significance when you have no hunger for the Word of God to impact your life during the week?"

Make every effort to set aside time for God each day. Ask Him to speak to you as you read a passage from the Bible. Expect Him to speak to you. Act on what you hear and learn. There is no form of authentic Christian living which ignores this simple yet essential exercise.

Until next week . . .

Devoted to Giving

But godliness actually is a means of great gain when accompanied by contentment. For we have brought nothing into the world, so we cannot take anything out of it either. If we have food and covering, with these we shall be content. But those who want to get rich fall into temptation and a snare and many foolish and harmful desires which plunge men into ruin and destruction. For the love of money is a root of all sorts of evil, and some by longing for it have wandered away from the faith and pierced themselves with many griefs. (1 Timothy 6:6-10)

Make sure that your character is free from the love of money, being content with what you have; for He Himself has said, "I WILL NEVER DESERT YOU, NOR WILL I EVER FORSAKE YOU." (Hebrews 13:5)

Money is god for a great many people. It is taken for granted that we should get as rich as we can and that the more we have the happier we shall be. An improved standard of living is the goal of Democrat and Republican alike, just as it is for governments and people around the world. In contrast with this, the Jesus we follow is remarkably unconcerned with the acquisition of wealth. There is no doctrinal opposition to money in the teachings of Jesus, but no slavery to it either. In short, there is nothing wrong with money—but there is a great deal wrong with the *love* of money.

What should be our attitude to money as followers of Jesus Christ?

1. *We shall not make money our goal.* Authentic wealth is not measured by our net worth nor our self-worth. Jesus Christ is our wealth, our provision and our abundance.

2. *We shall not trust in our money.* One of the most insidious dangers of wealth is that it tends to make men spiritually arrogant, independent and unwilling to rely on God for their needs. Whether we are rich or poor, we are all tempted to think that all would be well if we just had more money.

> Give me neither poverty nor riches;
> Feed me with the food that is my
>   portion,
> That I not be full and deny You and say,
>   "Who is the LORD?"
> Or that I not be in want and steal,
> And profane the name of my God.

> (Proverbs 30:8-9)

3. *We shall want to give.* This is part of the inner revolution that begins when the Holy Spirit enters our lives. So complete is our transformation in Christ that Paul can expect a thief to go from taking to giving without even a twelve-step program (see Ephesians 4:28)!

4. *We shall see ourselves as accountable to God for our use of money.* Scripture is clear:

> Tell them to use their money to do good. They should be rich in good works and should give happily to those in need, always being ready to share with others whatever God has given them. (1 Timothy 6:17-19, LB)

> Whether I have a lot of money or a little is immaterial. As a Christian I ought to give a portion of my income to God—the Jews gave a minimum of ten percent and I do not see how a Christian can give less. In the New Testament giving is not merely a duty. It is a highly personal demonstration of our love to the Lord—"for where your treasure is, there your heart will be also" (Matthew 6:21). For the Christian the issue is not giving; it is stewardship—the recognition that we act as the administrators of Another's possessions.

There is tragic irony in the fact that the average evangelical Christian tithes two percent of his income to God and pays thirty percent of his income in tax to Uncle Sam. Could it be that God is saying to the Church in the U.S., "Because you have trusted in money and withheld the tithe from Me, I will plunder your riches so that you will not see the gain"? Is it mere coincidence that taxes began to increase when the Church began to decrease the tithe? Think of what the Church could do for the poor, the illiterate, the migrant, the children, etc., if we tithed just ten percent. We would do well to question any spirituality, including our own, where the love and power of Jesus Christ has not triumphed over our spending and giving habits. The call to give is just as clear as the call to pray or the call to serve.

Until next week . . .

PART FOUR

Spirit-Filled

Jesus promised that the fullness of the Holy Spirit would be like rivers of living water flowing from within. I fear that too many of us have exchanged His simile of the "river" for one of a "puddle."

Filled with the Holy Spirit

When the day of Pentecost had come, they were all together in one place. And suddenly there came from heaven a noise like a violent rushing wind, and it filled the whole house where they were sitting. And there appeared to them tongues as of fire distributing themselves, and they rested on each one of them. And they were all filled with the Holy Spirit and began to speak with other tongues, as the Spirit was giving them utterance.

Now there were Jews living in Jerusalem, devout men from every nation under heaven. And when this sound occurred, the crowd came together, and were bewildered because each one of them was hearing them speak in his own language. They were amazed and astonished, saying, "Why, are not all these who are speaking Galileans? And how is it that we each hear them in our own language to which we were born? . . ."

And they all continued in amazement and great perplexity, saying to one another, "What does this mean?" (Acts 2:1-8, 12)

Almost all Christians that I know want to be full of the Holy Spirit, but many seem to deny their need to be filled. Yet surely this is still the great need among men today—for a powerful filling of the Spirit that will cause us to desire God, hunger for His Word, be fervent in prayer, boldly share our faith, obey His commands, love those we find unlovable, use our gifts to build up the local church, give liberally and expect Him to act wondrously in our time.

It goes without saying that such a filling of the Spirit that could accomplish this will also empower us to heal the sick, deliver the captive and reconcile relationships.

Anyone who wants to know how he can be filled with the Spirit must first desire to be filled. This is not as simple as it sounds. A.W. Tozer comments,

> Are you sure that you want to be possessed by a spirit other than your own . . . even though that spirit be the pure Spirit of God? . . . That Spirit, if He ever possesses you, will be the Lord of your life! . . .
>
> Are you sure that you want your personality to be taken over by One who will expect obedience to the written and living

Word? Are you sure that you want your personality to be taken over by One who will not tolerate the self sins? . . . Self-love, self-confidence, self-righteousness, self-admiration, self-aggrandizement and self-pity are under the interdiction of God Almighty, and He cannot send His mighty Spirit to possess the heart where these things are.

Again, I ask you if you desire to have your personality taken over by One who stands in sharp opposition to the world's easy ways. No tolerance of evil, no smiling at crooked jokes, no laughing off things God hates. The Spirit of God, if He takes over, will bring you into opposition to the world just as Jesus was brought into op-position to it. The world crucified Jesus because they couldn't stand Him! . . . Are you sure, brother? You want His help, yes; you want a lot of His benefits, yes; but are you willing to go with Him in His opposi-tion to the easygoing ways of the world? If you are not, you needn't apply for any-thing more than you have, because you don't want Him; you only think you do!

Again, are you sure that you need to be filled? Can't you get along the way you are? You have been doing fairly well: You pray, you read your Bible, you give to mis-sions, you enjoy singing hymns, you thank God you don't drink or gamble or attend theaters, that you are honest, that you have prayer at home. You are glad about all this. Can't you get along like that? Are you sure you need any more than that? . . .

But maybe you feel in your heart that you just can't go on as you are, that the level of spirituality to which you know yourself called is way beyond you. If you feel that there is something that you must have or your heart will never be satisfied, that there are levels of spirituality, mystic deeps and heights of spiritual communion, purity and power that you have never known, that there is fruit which you know you should bear and do not, victory which you know you should have and have not—I would say, "Come on," because God has something for you.[5]

While I shy away from formulas, I would suggest that we can be filled with the Holy Spirit as we:

Surrender: "Therefore I urge you, brethren, by the mercies of God, to present your bodies a living and holy sacrifice, acceptable to God, which is your spiritual service of worship. And do not be conformed to this world, but be transformed by the renewing of your mind, so that you may prove what the will of God is, that which is good and acceptable and perfect" (Romans 12:1-2).

Ask: "If you then, being evil, know how to give good gifts to your children, how much more will your heavenly Father give the Holy Spirit to those who ask Him?" (Luke 11:13).

Obey: "And we are witnesses of these things; and so is the Holy Spirit, whom God has given to those who obey Him" (Acts 5:32).

Believe: "This is the only thing I want to find out from you: did you receive the Spirit by the works of the Law, or by hearing with faith?" (Galatians 3:2).

Dwight Moody was pointedly asked, "Have you been filled with the Holy Spirit?" After a moment's pause to think he replied, "Yes, but I leak." A spiritless faith will never deliver the realities we long or labor toward.

Until next week . . .

The Testimony of the Holy Spirit

You will receive power when the Holy Spirit comes on you; and you will be my witnesses in Jerusalem, and in all Judea and Samaria, and to the ends of the earth. (Acts 1:8, NIV)

For this reason we must pay much closer attention to what we have heard, so that we do not drift far away from it. . . . How will we escape if we neglect so great a salvation? After it was at the first spoken through the Lord, it was confirmed to us by those who heard, God also testifying with them, both by signs and wonders and by various miracles and by gifts of the Holy Spirit according to His own will. (Hebrews 2:1-4)

The primary purpose of the Holy Spirit is to empower you to be a witness to Jesus Christ and the salvation that comes in His

name. In other words, to be a witness for Jesus
Christ, we first need a witness. The New Testament
describes this witness as the baptism of the Holy
Spirit, the empowering of the Holy Spirit or the filling of the Holy Spirit. You must not expect your experience of the Holy Spirit's witness to be identical
with another, nor should any single experience or
manifestation be projected as normative for all.
There are various and diverse experiences of the
Holy Spirit. Sometimes He comes upon you gently
and other times as a mighty torrent of conviction
and strength. What is normative is that the Holy
Spirit's coming is a tangible, albeit sometimes inef-
fable, experience in the life of a person because He
comes to bear witness.

His witness brings a fresh awareness of the presence of God. The Holy Spirit makes real to us the
promises which we have embraced by faith. His
love, His grace, His majesty and His strength are
not merely the lyrics of choruses and hymns any-
more—they are realities of God's empowering
presence in our lives. Faith is no longer merely the
will to believe or a cognitive affirmation of doctrinal truth. Instead faith becomes, through the
witness of the Holy Spirit, like a living umbilical
cord between the seen and the unseen, nourishing
and sustaining our life in Him.

His witness provokes in us a fresh sense of awe
in the presence of God. The men of Scripture
who meet God never refer to Him tritely or in
over-familiar terms. Their intimacy with Him is
never an excuse for presumptuous speech or be-

havior. Instead, men in whom the Spirit bears witness have a deep reverence for the Lord. They recognize the gravity of their sin, the duplicity of their ways, the great disparity between their humanity and His glory, greatness and majesty.

His witness brings the assurance of God's love. The Holy Spirit's testimony gives to us the overwhelming knowledge of God's love through Jesus Christ. The Spirit powerfully proclaims to the soul of the believer what He said to His own Son, "You are My beloved Son, in You I am well pleased" (Luke 3:22). Paul simply described it this way: "The Spirit Himself testifies with our spirit that we are children of God" (Romans 8:16).

Thomas Goodwin, a Puritan living in the seventeenth century described it this way: A man is walking with his little child. The child knows that he is the child of his father; he knows that his father loves him; he rejoices in that love; and he is happy in it. There is no uncertainty about his relationship with his father—but suddenly the father, moved by some impulse known only to him, takes hold of his child and picks him up. He lifts him through the air above him and then lowers him so that their eyes meet. He tussles his hair, squeezes his arms, embraces him and then sets him down and they continue walking on together. The child knew before that his father loved him, and he knew that he was his child. Nevertheless this loving embrace, the serendipitous joy of being swung through the air, the meeting of their eyes and the tussle of his hair all communicate this love in extraordinary ways. The relationship is unchanged and yet the child is assured in extraordinary ways. Such is the witness of the Holy Spirit.

The witness of the Holy Spirit is not a once-for-all-time experience. He is God's continuing gift to us for all time. He is God's personal witness to us so that we might bear witness to Him. May we all be empowered by the witness of God in Jesus' name.

Until next week . . .

You Shall Receive Power . . .

But you will receive power when the Holy Spirit has come upon you. . . . (Acts 1:8)

We have this treasure in jars of clay to show that this all-surpassing power is from God and not from us. (2 Corinthians 4:7, NIV)

Thousands of men since Jesus have proven a very simple truth: Real power lies in the majesty of God's eternal light and might moving upon the consciences and minds of men through the Holy Spirit. His power is not impersonal or ambiguous. It is the presence, power and personal love of Jesus Christ tangibly filling our lives today.

Do not be distracted by unbalanced or complicated teachings regarding this very simple promise of Jesus: "You will receive power" (Acts 1:8). When you receive Jesus at conversion you receive the Holy Spirit. And when you enthrone Jesus you receive the fullness of the Holy Spirit. The promise is really very simple:

Receive Christ—receive the Holy Spirit.

Enthrone Christ—receive the fullness of the Spirit.

We receive Christ once for all time but we must enthrone Him daily. I am afraid it is the second half of the equation that is frequently absent from much of today's teaching. The Christian life is not a lifelong therapy session wherein Jesus counsels and guides us to know ourselves better. The Christian life is the promise of fullness in which we enthrone Christ and know Him more fully. Furthermore, there is no reason why we should not grow in our experience of this fullness that our Father offers us in Jesus.

Here are four simple steps we can all take to prepare and enjoy this fullness of life that Jesus offers us:

1. *Let us try to realize as fully as we can that our sins and ineffectiveness hurt the One we love.* Our sin matters deeply to God. It does not merely provoke His wrath—it moves Him to act out His love toward us. Consider the pain we feel when we see those we love dearly falling into lives of selfishness, self-indulgence and isolation. How much more will our God—Father, Son and Holy Spirit—feel when He looks upon us! Our supreme motivation for seeking the fullness of God should be Christ's love for us. We exclaim with the apostle Paul, "Christ's love compels us" (2 Corinthians 5:14, NIV).

2. *Let us surrender ourselves utterly to the master-ing power and love of the Holy Spirit.* This should not only be our act at the moment of conversion but also the act, repeated often, of a will which wants to make absolutely sure that it is abandoned to God. The Christian life is a serendipitous journey wherein we dili-gently search out and discover the will of God as it is revealed to us through His Word, by His Spirit and through daily opportunities He opens up to us.

3. *Let us repent fully of sins committed against other people and put right, to the utmost of our ability, what may be wrong between others and ourselves.* Let us make all the adjustments that need to be made for this new life regardless of the cost to us. Yet, in a spirit of love and for-bearance, let us walk in the Spirit of love where all others are concerned.

4. *Let us die to ourselves.* Jesus said that those who hunger and thirst for righteousness shall be filled (Matthew 5:6). So we must die to our-selves and the virtues we glory in—our prayers, our earnestness, our knowledge of the Bible, our witnessing, our Christian work, our attain-ments, our past experience, our anything—so we may begin to know the true death of self and union with the crucified Savior. We fool our-selves if we think these virtues have value apart from the cross of Christ where we too must die. We must consent to and glory in the fact that

our sinful nature was nailed to the cross with Christ 2,000 years ago. And it is still there with Him today (Galatians 2:20).

Let us receive all that He has promised to give and enthrone Him as our King . . .

I take salvation full and free
  Through Him who gave His life for me;
He undertakes my all to be—
  I take, He undertakes.

I take the promised Holy Ghost,
  I take the power of Pentecost
To fill me to the uttermost—
  I take, He undertakes.

I take Thee, blessed Lord,
  I give myself to Thee;
And Thou, according to Thy Word,
  Dost undertake for me.[6]

Until next week . . .

A Sign of the Spirit

. . . Be filled with the Spirit. Speak to one another with psalms, hymns and spiritual songs. Sing and make music in your heart to the Lord, always giving thanks to God the Father for everything, in the name of our Lord Jesus Christ. (Ephesians 5:18-20, NIV)

These verses present four consequences of being filled with the Holy Spirit. *First, a Holy Spirit-filled person is one who loves to worship God.* You will recognize him by his intensity in prayer, his attentiveness to God's presence, his exuberant praise, his expressive joy and his gracious freedom.

One of the most frequent and wonderful impressions visitors to our worship celebrations describe is the joy, beauty and freedom they perceive as our congregation worships. On one occasion a woman commented that she noticed one of the men worshiping with his eyes open. She went on to say,

"His countenance possessed joy and wonderment. I was sure he was looking at someone so I just had to follow his gaze. The way he looked, I really expected to see Jesus standing there!"

Second, the Holy Spirit-filled person does not stop worshiping when the church service is completed. His worship continues throughout the week as he sings and makes music in his heart to the Lord. Worship songs, hymns, scriptures and God-honoring images and ideas regularly fill his mind throughout the week. He will frequently be aware that this wellspring of adoration is not his own creation but instead it is being "poured" into him by the Spirit of God Himself!

Third, the Holy Spirit-filled person is not a worshiping "lone ranger." He looks forward to praising God with others and strives to encourage and release vital worship in his church. Like King David, he exclaims, "Glorify the LORD with me; let us exalt his name together" (Psalm 34:3, NIV). His enthusiasm is contagious and he remains steadfast in his resolve to gather with other believers even when inconvenienced by weather, travel, vocation or even family.

Nothing excites me more than when people share with me that they attend our church because of the worship. Do I desire to shepherd, lead and serve the congregation I pastor through the message I bring each Sunday? Yes! Do I want to be affirmed as a good Bible teacher? Yes! But I am a realist too. I recognize that when God is not first loved and adored there can be no heartfelt expectancy, no authentic responsiveness and no transforming impact. It has always been so with the people of God. The best seed in the world cannot grow where the soil is ill-prepared to receive it.

Fourth, the Holy Spirit-filled person expresses his trust in God for every situation through thanksgiving and praise. The Spirit-filled person knows that he is not called to praise God for evil or tragedy. He also understands that circumstances do not judge the presence or absence of God nor the verity of His ways. Through worship the Spirit-filled person is free to give thanks to God because he knows with his mind and in his heart that God is in control and loves him as his own.

Descartes epitomized the Enlightenment when he postulated, "I think, therefore I am." The Holy Spirit-filled person counters, "I worship, therefore I am." Human identity is not formed by our cognitive capacity to contemplate or ponder. Identity is formed in the incendiary crucible of worship. There the Holy Spirit apprehends, fills and vitally reveals to each person that he is made in the image of God and destined for glory.

What would our lives and congregations look like if these four signs of the Holy Spirit were abundantly evident?

Until next week . . .

PART FIVE

Vibrant

Vibrancy is the art of carrying God's "new age" fullness into the "old age" emptiness in which we live. What hunger is in relation to food, vibrancy is in relation to life.

A Man Made New

*Therefore if anyone is in Christ, he is a
new creature; the old things passed
away; behold, new things have come.
(2 Corinthians 5:17)*

Therefore if anyone . . .
  an old one or young one . . .
    a rich one or poor one . . .
      an extraordinary one or an average one . . .
        an athletic one or a clumsy one . . .
          a clever one or a dim-witted one . . .
        a blue-collar one or a white-collar one . . .
      a leader-one or a follower-one . . .
    a passive one or an aggressive one . . .
  a married one or a single one . . .

Is in Christ . . .
forgiven . . .
  liberated . . .
    reconciled . . .
      restored . . .
        called . . .
      adopted . . .
    gifted . . .

loved . . .
filled . . .

The old . . .
the primitive . . .
the antiquated . . .
the expired . . .
the worn-out . . .
the used-up . . .
the obsolete . . .
the decayed . . .
the out-of-date . . .
the run-dry . . .

Things . . .
pride . . .
lying . . .
fear . . .
lust . . .
envy . . .
greed . . .
brokenness . . .
unforgiveness . . .
estrangement . . .
prejudice . . .
loneliness . . .

Passed away . . .
surpassed . . .
passed over . . .
exceeded . . .
gone by . . .
nullified . . .

Behold . . .
Look!
Take notice!
Listen up!
Pay attention!
Check this out!
You've got to see this!
You're not going to believe this, BUT—

New . . .
the unexpected . . .
the unfamiliar . . .
the wonderful . . .
the unforeseen surprise . . .
the implausible, but true, joy

Things . . .
a new Savior
a new covenant . . .
a new kingdom . . .
a new Spirit . . .
a new promise . . .
a new grace . . .
a new life . . .
a new name . . .
a new nature . . .
a new courage . . .
a new song . . .
a new strength . . .
a new hope . . .
a new love . . .
a new joy . . .
a new future . . .

Have come . . .
   has arrived . . .
      has landed . . .
         has succeeded . . .
      has triumphed . . .
is here to stay . . .

Dear ones in Christ, I have written this amplified translation to remind you of a simple and life-changing New Testament truth. In Jesus Christ, you have been made new. Therefore you are now fundamentally incompatible with any remnant of the old which you continue to give place to, embrace or flirt with. Most bouts of spiritual lethargy, compromise, stagnation, futility and oppression stem from a spiritual naiveté that thinks we can, by grace, enjoy a new life in Christ while remaining indifferent to the patterns, lifestyle and behaviors of the old one.

In the New Testament the "new" surpasses the "old," rendering it archaic, primitive and obsolete (see Hebrews 8:13 as one example). You cannot enjoy the newness of your life in Christ while clinging to the old any more than you can replace your car engine's spark plugs with matches and expect it to run—let alone start!

The Holy Spirit speaks to us through this verse, challenging each of us to let go of what He has determined must pass away from our lives.

We can make no better start than to take a moment to . . .

    consider the vestiges of the old
      you still cling to . . .
        ask the Lord to have it pass away and
        prayerfully consider what steps
          you will begin taking TODAY!

Until next week . . .

Your Life Is Destined to Be Fruitful

"I am the true vine, and my Father is the gardener. He cuts off every branch in me that bears no fruit, while every branch that does bear fruit he prunes so that it will be even more fruitful. You are already clean because of the word I have spoken to you. Remain in me, and I will remain in you. No branch can bear fruit by itself; it must remain in the vine. Neither can you bear fruit unless you remain in me.

I am the vine; you are the branches. If a man remains in me and I in him, he will bear much fruit; apart from me you can do nothing." (John 15:1-5, NIV)

There are certain passages of Scripture that are guaranteed to quell the schemes of a godly person. These passages are intrusions into our spiritual comfort zones. They unsettle us with their observations and convict us by their bluntness. It is not that such passages are intended to condemn us as much as they reflect the kind of truth for which we rearrange our lives.

In this passage Jesus tells us very clearly that:

- ✿ He is the true vine.
- ✿ Our Father is the gardener.
- ✿ We are branches that are intended to bear much fruit.

So far so good. But He goes on to say:

- ✿ Some branches will be cut off because they do not bear any fruit.
- ✿ Branches will be pruned so they can bear even more fruit.

The good news is every branch that remains in the vine has the capacity to bear fruit. The bad news is if I bear no fruit I will get "cut off" and if I bear much fruit I will get "pruned." This sounds perilously close to a "lose-lose" situation! Yet I do not think that Jesus' words here can be pressed to apply to issues of salvation and eternal damnation since both kinds of branches begin connected to the vine (15:2). Instead I think He is describing the reality of Christian growth and the way that God prepares a disciple to be useful to His work in the world today.

Jesus is here speaking of two conditions. The first is the presence of branches that are dead or diseased and whose continuing presence will threaten its viability for future growth and production. These branches cannot be tolerated. They must be decisively cut off if your goal is fruitfulness. Sin, when exposed or recognized, cannot be tolerated and flirted with. What our culture calls normal the Lord frequently calls sin. It must be decisively addressed through repentance, the acceptance of God's grace and the power of the Holy Spirit to repudiate its attraction and to renounce its power. Diseased branches must be cut off to maintain the health of the plant.

The second condition Jesus describes is a fruitful branch that is pruned back. The gardener prunes a branch in order to force it to rest. This forced dormancy is necessary because without it the plant will keep attempting to grow and will exhaust itself over the long run.[7] Thus there is never, from the perspective of a fruitful plant, a good time to be pruned. Pruning is always problematic because you cannot be pruned and be fruitful at the same time. Pruning is always painful, intrusive and inconvenient because the ambition to grow and be fruitful will not naturally curtail itself. That is why we need the Gardener.

Different plants will be cared for in different ways. Some fruit trees are pruned very slightly because they bear their fruit on old wood (experience?) while others are pruned quite severely because they must bear their fruit on new wood (repentance?). Yet we can rest confident in knowing that we have a good Gardener who knows how to care and grow every plant.

If you want to bear much fruit for the Gardener you must be willing to have that which is diseased, dead *and* fruitful cut off. The Gardener must have the freedom to trim, shape, direct and feed you. There is no other way.

Until next week . . .

Obedience Is Our Cornerstone

The word of the LORD came to me,
   saying,
"Before I formed you in the womb I knew
   you,
before you were born I set you apart;
I appointed you as a prophet to the
   nations." (Jeremiah 1:4-5, NIV)

"If you love Me, you will keep My com-
mandments." (John 14:15)

bedience is the cornerstone of a Christian faith that is alive and compelling. Faith without obedience will lack both integrity and substance. In 1937, on the eve of the Nazi horror, Dietrich Bonhoeffer wrote, "Only he who believes obeys. Only he who obeys believes." Disobedience is faithlessness in action. People do not disobey their Savior out of love; we do so out of mistrust, fear, greed, covetousness, pride or a will to power. Disobedience is never undertaken as a step of faith—it settles for the sure (secure?) thing. When we choose disobedience we are repudiating

Christ's kingly role and choosing the world.
(Compare Paul's reference to Demas in these passages: Colossians 4:14 and Philemon 1:24 with 2
Timothy 4:10.) A disobedient Christian is an
AWOL Christian. Beware: Such people are unpredictable and not trustworthy. Do you think someone who ignores his Savior's counsel will not do
the same to you?

Obedience is an affair of the heart before it
ever becomes a crisis of conduct. An obedient
person is one who is responsive to God's Word
and ready to do His bidding. The prophet Jeremiah clearly exemplifies this. When the people of
God were in a desperate situation, God answered
their prayers with an anxious, inexperienced
young man—a country boy from a poor village,
with no startling gifts, very conscious of his
weakness and desperately in need of love and
understanding. Surely God had picked the
wrong man—Jeremiah certainly thought so!

" 'Ah, Sovereign LORD,' [he] said, 'I do not know
how to speak; I am only a child.' But the LORD said
to [him], . . . 'I am with you and will rescue you. . . .
I have put my words in your mouth' " (Jeremiah
1:6-9, NIV).

Why did God choose Jeremiah? It was for one
reason only—he was willing to obey.

Mark this well: If a person is willing to obey
God then
> weakness,
>> inexperience,
>>> age or
>>>> lack of ability

do not matter because God's Spirit within that person is more than enough for every situation. Do you believe this?

Throughout the history of the Church, God has taken young, inexperienced people and equipped them by His Spirit for great work. Think of David, Samuel, Daniel, John the Baptist and Timothy. Calvin wrote the first edition of his *Institutes* at the age of twenty-four; Wesley founded Methodism at twenty-five; Ian Murray McCheyne, who shook Scotland with his preaching, died at twenty-nine. Oswald Chambers, author of the best-selling devotional book of all time, *My Utmost for His Highest*, was dead by forty-one.

Another young man once heard someone remark, "The world has yet to see what God will do with a man fully consecrated to Him." The young man stood up and replied, "By the Holy Spirit, I'll be that man." His name was Dwight L. Moody and thousands turned to Christ through his ministry.

In these critical days, God is calling out and looking for people with obedient hearts. Will you be such a person?

Until next week . . .

Build a Life-Giving Church

For we are God's fellow workers; you are . . . God's building. (1 Corinthians 3:9)

You also, as living stones, are being built up as a spiritual house. . . . (1 Peter 2:5)

Followers of Jesus Christ do not go to church. Followers of Jesus Christ *are* the Church. God's building is no longer a temple; it is a people called and set apart by Him. God's building is not a holy place; God's building is a holy people. God's building is not complete: It is still under construction—but one day it will comprise all peoples, tribes and tongues.

Remember, to the untrained eye most buildings under construction look like a terrible mess until the last stage is reached. The same is true with the Church. The dust and dirt, chaos and confusion may make it hard to believe that this could really be the temple of God. Yet, if we have faith and patience, we will see that the Architect and Builder is hard at work and knows very well what He is doing—He is building us into "God's building." The apostle Peter observed, "You also, like living stones, are being built into a spiritual house" (1 Peter 2:5, NIV). This has two immediate consequences for every follower of Jesus Christ.

First, the Church is made up of "living" stones, not cold, inanimate ones. The building God is constructing is alive to Christ and responsive to His call. It is not ostentatious nor pretentious. It is not constructed for the privileged few or other "bricks" just like us. The bricks are not fixed or inflexible. The building of the Lord is a multipurpose structure designed to be the living reference point for the arrival of God's kingdom. While this analogy may be an architectural impossibility, it reflects God's design for His Church today. He is building one Church—united, interdependent and alive— whose impact upon the world shall be contingent upon the stones' willingness to be built together by the Lord into the house of His choosing.

Second, individual Christians are not the "building," we are the brick! Individual followers of Jesus Christ must not echo the proclamation of Henry David Thoreau, "I am my own church." Time and again Scripture exhorts us to "not give up meeting together, as some are in the habit of doing" (Hebrews 10:25, NIV). Nothing guts the momentum of a Christian fellowship faster than sporadic participation and attendance. How will the bricks be built together if they remain scattered and distant? Scripture is very clear: God expects our faith to be lived out in community. He intends us to be contributors, not merely consumers—to do otherwise is to deprive and weaken God's house. He desires us to be a vital part of something that is much greater than we can ever imagine or implement alone.

The foundation and cornerstone of God's house is Jesus Christ. His personal oversight ensures that the house will be radiant, responsive and resilient. It is His life which sustains the whole and gives shape to what is built. "In him the whole building is joined together and rises to become a holy temple in the Lord" (Ephesians 2:21, NIV). Does your commitment to Jesus Christ reflect His high priority and design for the Church? Does your lifestyle reflect a priority for worship and participation in your local congregation? Don't deprive the Church of the gifts God has given you.

Until next week . . .

PART SIX

Upright

Integrity is not who you are when no one is looking. This understanding confuses privacy with honor. The fact is that history is nothing more than the record of all encounters between integrity and circumstance.

The Uniqueness
of Christian Integrity

Now when [Jesus] saw the crowds, he went up on a mountainside and sat down. His disciples came to him, and he began to teach them, saying,

"Blessed are the poor in spirit. . . . Blessed are those who mourn. . . . Blessed are the meek. . . . Blessed are those who hunger and thirst for righteousness. . . . Blessed are the merciful. . . . Blessed are the pure in heart, for they will see God. Blessed are the peacemakers. . . . Blessed are those who are persecuted because of righteousness. . . .

Blessed are you when people insult you, persecute you and falsely say all kinds of evil against you. . . .

You are the salt of the earth. . . .

You are the light of the world. . . .

And when you pray, do not be like the hypocrites. . . .

Do not worry. . . .

But everyone who hears these words of
mine and does not put them into practice
. . . ." (Matthew 5:1-6:5, 25; 7:26, NIV)

*T*he Sermon on the Mount contrasts two
ways of living before God. One way mea-
sures faithfulness by what we do and the
other by who we are. In short, the Sermon on the
Mount is about integrity that is distinctly Christian.
Every sentence bears the conviction that who we
are on the inside matters immensely to Jesus because there is no inherent relationship between
what we do and who we truly are. A person may go
to church, sing the songs and read his Bible, but
never have the essential poverty of spirit that God
blesses with salvation, love and strength (Matthew
5:3). A man may not cheat on his spouse, but his fidelity is compromised by his obsession with lust
and sexual fantasies of every kind (5:27-30). A
person may pray eloquently in front of others, but
God knows that it is not an expression of faith but a
will to impress, influence and manipulate (6:5-
15).

Christian integrity is distinct. Philosophers suggest that integrity means living life according to a
consistent set of principles—but surely consistency
is the wrong criterion because one could then say
that Hitler had integrity! Christian integrity is less a
state and more an exercise of living, discerning,
loving, reflecting and doing that is inspired, em-

powered and exemplified by the person and power of Jesus.

There are three basic steps to pursuing a life of Christian integrity.[8] *The first step is to spend the time to discern the presence of Jesus in our lives.* Our relationship with Him is our foundation for understanding right and wrong, good and evil, commitment and hypocrisy. Therefore prayer, Bible study and quiet reflection are essential disciplines for those seeking a life of integrity. Christian integrity is distinct because we live according to our relationship with Jesus—He alone is our living "set of principles" that we seek to be consistent with.

The second step to a life of Christian integrity is to struggle to live according to our relationship of faith in Jesus Christ. Salvation is a free gift, but the Christian life is a lifetime-encompassing challenge. We pursue a life of integrity when we are willing to fight, strive and persevere to live in a manner that reflects the life of Jesus Christ within us. This means that a life of Christian integrity will be counterintuitive. We will love those whom Jesus loves, although we may initially feel no natural attraction; we will take actions that will advance Christ but do little for us; we will risk the loss of favor and esteem to live out our life in Christ.

The third and often overlooked step to a life of Christian integrity requires us to be open and emphatic about Who and what we are living by—to say why we do the things we are doing or believe the things we are believing. Witness is an essential ingredient to Christian integrity because integrity, as a lifestyle, can never be separated from the person and power of Jesus Christ. We live, believe, act, relate, love, hope, judge and yearn the way we do because of Jesus. Christian integrity mandates that we bear witness to Him because it is only His person that can make sense of the life of integrity that we struggle to achieve.

Until next week. . .

The Hallmarks of Integrity

Again, you have heard that it was said to the people long ago, "Do not break your oath, but keep the oaths you have made to the Lord." But I tell you, Do not swear at all: either by heaven, for it is God's throne; or by the earth, for it is his footstool; or by Jerusalem, for it is the city of the Great King. And do not swear by your head, for you cannot make even one hair white or black. Simply let your "Yes" be "Yes," and your "No," "No"; anything beyond this comes from the evil one. (Matthew 5:33-37, NIV)

having daily reminds me of two important truths for living strategically. First, if I want to let my face "go" there is only one thing I have to do: nothing! Doing nothing is not an option for strategic living. Second, shaving requires that I make a daily choice—to shave or not to shave, that is the question! Living strategically requires that I make choices each day that will honor the call of Jesus Christ upon my life. Every day offers a myriad of opportunities for me to "choose for [myself] this day whom [I] will serve" (Joshua 24:15). These two simple truths can be applied to almost every area of my life where I sense God is calling me to develop and mature.

Biblical integrity requires a daily decision on my part to ask the Holy Spirit to shape my life in such a way that there may be (the hope of) continuity between my "inside" and my "outside." Integrity will not just happen. The quest for integrity requires me to do something. The prize I seek demands that I yield my life—my choices, my passions, my hopes and my convictions—to Jesus, twenty-four hours each day, seven days a week, fifty-two weeks a year, for the rest of my life.

Years ago I developed this acrostic to help me in my quest for integrity . . .

- **I**ntegrity is **I**ntentional. Every day I must make decisions that will cultivate the discipline of integrity.
- i**N**tegrity is **N**ot self-authenticating. I will never be able to boast that I am a man of integrity. It is an estimation of my character which only others can make. I am skeptical of anyone who could confidently say, "I am a person of integrity," just as I am when someone proudly tells me, "I have the gift of humility!"

- inTegrity takes Time. Time to pray, time to grow, time to mature, time to reflect, time to anticipate.
- intEgrity Embraces all areas of our lives. Both the secret and the public fall under the purview of integrity.
- inteGrity takes Grace. If I do not appropriate the power and experience of God's grace, the quest for integrity will quickly degenerate into a new legalism that will quench the power of the Holy Spirit in my life.
- integRity requires Relationships. It is not lived out in a vacuum. Integrity is forged in the daily crucible of our community, our vocation, our family and our friendships.
- integrIty will challenge the Idols of our imagination. Integrity serves the truth. Therefore it is impartial and objective. It will not turn a blind eye toward my hidden sin nor consider trivial what the world considers normal (i.e., lust).
- integriTy tells the Truth—half-truths, gossip, lies, innuendo, coercion and manipulation are not options in the quest for integrity.
- integritY takes You! No one else can fill in for you or choose integrity on your behalf. Neither can you remain inactive and rely on someone else to act with integrity. As Churchill was fond of quoting, "All it takes

for evil to triumph is for good men to do nothing."

I hear the call of the Father to pursue integrity in David's charge to Samuel: "So be strong, show yourself a man, and observe what the LORD your God requires: Walk in his ways, and keep his decrees and commands" (1 Kings 2:2-3, NIV).

This is the integrity I seek. Will you join me?

Until next week . . .

Ten Steps to Christian Integrity

I know, my God, that you test the heart and are pleased with integrity. . . . (1 Chronicles 29:17, NIV)

ntegrity is not mere truth-telling. It is a pattern of living in Christ that is unbroken, whole and unified by the direct continuity between the "inner" man and the "outer" man, whose words and behaviors may be witnessed by all. Integrity is the virtue of a life surrendered to Him and therefore free to live for His honor. This means that a man of integrity possesses congruity between his private self ("hidden with Christ") and his public persona ("you shall be my witness"). A man of integrity recognizes that he is ultimately living his life for an audience of "One" and therefore strives to give "his utmost for His highest."

How can we cultivate integrity in our lives? Where can we turn to discover a model of integrity which is distinctly Christian and inspired by God Himself? I would suggest to you that the Ten Commandments are a good place to start (Exodus 20:1-17). Here we are challenged and encouraged in ten crucial areas that are essential to a lifestyle of integrity that pleases the heart of God. (In fact, I think they could be retitled "Every Person's Guide to Integrity.")

1. *The Affection of Our Hearts* ("no other gods before Me"): Do I love God—Father, Son and Holy Spirit? Do I seek to make Him preeminent in my life, my loves and my ambitions?

2. *The Imagination of Our Minds* ("no idols"): Is my "God" little more than the projection of my thoughts and fears? Are my imagination and fantasies consistent with the images of God revealed in Scripture or do they indicate that someone or something else comes first?

3. *The Expression of Our Mouths* ("not using God's name in vain"): Do my words reflect reverence or irreverence? Is there congruity between my "God-talk" and the current state of my relationship with God? Is my walk with the Lord as intimate as the walk I publicly portray?

4. *The Reflection of Our Trust* ("keeping the Sabbath holy"): Does my use of time indicate trust and reliance upon God's provision? Do I see time as a gift to be given back to God? Do I trust God enough to take time off?

5. *The Honor of Parents* ("honor your father and mother"): Do I respect my parents or do I blame them for my problems? How can I say I will love my neighbor when I cannot honor my parents?

6. *The Sanctity of Human Life* ("you shall not murder"): Jesus said that anger against your brother is like committing murder in your heart (see Matthew 5:21-22). How can I bring the love of Christ to others when there is so much violence in my own heart? Do I experience and express the mercy, peace, love and reconciliation that Jesus brings? Do I honor life?

7. *A Healthy Esteem for Marriage/Sexual Intimacy* ("do not commit adultery"): Do I honor marriage? Do I contend for God's plan for marriage and sexual intimacy? Do I allow myself to be aroused by pornography or sexual imagery? Am I flirtatious with the opposite sex? Do I consider divorce an option?

8. *The Respect for Property* ("do not steal"): Do I steal "time" that belongs to my job, family or friends? Am I responsible with my financial obligations? Do I rob God of the tithe He is due? Do I rob others of their reputation through gossip, innuendo or slanderous speech?

9. *The Veneration of Truthfulness* ("do not bear false witness")—this is both judicial and social: Who am I when no one is looking? Am I a person of my word? Am I willing to take responsibility for my mistakes and failures? Do I fabri-

cate excuses when I feel under pressure? Do the ends justify the means?

10. *The Cultivation of Contentment* ("do not covet"): Do I direct my desires toward contentment in Christ? Do I seek contentment through the acquisition of things or people? Do I think that relationships, money and/or things will bring me contentment? Does my spending reflect accountability and contentment? Does my lifestyle reflect the freedom of simplicity or the chaos of worldliness?

Until next week . . .

Sexual Integrity (Part 1)

But you will receive power when the Holy Spirit comes on you. (Acts 1:8, NIV)

We have this treasure in jars of clay to show that this all-surpassing power is from God and not from us. (2 Corinthians 4:7, NIV)

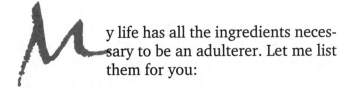y life has all the ingredients necessary to be an adulterer. Let me list them for you:

1. I love Jesus.
2. I love my wife, Carol.
3. I love my four girls: Alison, Catherine, Bethany and Danielle.
4. I love the congregation I pastor.
5. It is my singular desire to live in such a manner as to honor my God and Savior, honor my wife and family and honor the family of God.

These may not sound like the values that lead to adultery, but they are—for this simple reason.

There is no necessary relationship between the choice to commit adultery and values a man may say he holds dear. Nearly all of the Christian men I have met who have committed adultery did so because they denied two fundamental realities of the male temperament.

1. Men have a marvelous capacity to disassociate long-term values for immediate gratification.
2. Men allow personal attraction toward other women to lead to arousal.

I remember the incident that first convicted me that marital fidelity was a spiritual discipline and a covenant that I needed to make to the Lord.

My wife, Carol, and I enjoyed a wonderful honeymoon in San Francisco and the Lake Tahoe area. It was a precious time to enjoy our friendship, to walk, to play and to enjoy the intimate sexual union God was blessing. There was no need for us to feel either shame or embarrassment before God or one another. I could sense God's pleasure amidst our own.

One week later we moved into a small two-bedroom house in Spokane, Washington. I was completing my undergraduate work and Carol was completing her teaching credential. I was working at that time as assistant chaplain at Whitworth College where I oversaw the campus interns. One of the interns was a senior, and older, like me. She was also very attractive. She met me one evening in my office to review her plans for one of the dorms. I quickly became aware that I was not paying attention to what she was talking about. Instead I found myself reflecting on how exceptionally attractive she was!

I began to break out in a cold sweat once I realized the direction my mind was taking (a mere three weeks after my wedding day!). I looked down at my watch, feigned surprise and lied as I blurted out that I was late to a meeting that I had forgotten about! I stood up and ran out of my office like Joseph fleeing Potiphar's wife. Except she was not the problem—I was.

I ran to one of my secret places on campus and hid myself. I cried out to God, "I have only been married three weeks and already I am an adulterer! O God, have mercy on me and take away these feelings." What happened next completely surprised me. The Lord spoke to me very clearly, "I will not take these feelings away from you. I will help you to master them and allow them to enrich your life as I intended them to."

God has been faithful to His word. I have enjoyed tremendous liberty. But I have never forgotten that day I learned more about myself than I wanted to know.

Here are some very simple steps that God has inspired me to take as a result of that incident:

1. I have made a covenant with the Lord to be faithful to Carol. Each day I take a fresh look at my wedding band and remember the life it calls me to lead before the Lord, Carol, my children and our extended community.

2. I have some very close friends with whom I have made a covenant to be faithful to my wife, honest with my use of money, diligent in my pursuit of Jesus Christ and militant in my quest for personal purity.
3. I take time to pray for Carol every day and extol specific virtues she possesses before the Lord.
4. I find the freedom to share about Carol whenever appropriate in conversations with others.

This allows me to affirm and, more importantly, remember my love, loyalty and respect for her. It is interesting to note that in the Old Testament a relationship is jeopardized every time a person or people begin to forget.

There can be no integrity where there is no passion for fidelity in our body, mind and spirit. We would do well to delight in the wife of our youth and to remember her well before the Lord and others throughout our days . . .

Until next week . . .

Sexual Integrity (Part 2)

You have heard that it was said, "Do not commit adultery." But I tell you that anyone who looks at a woman lustfully has already committed adultery with her in his heart. If your right eye causes you to sin, gouge it out and throw it away. It is better for you to lose one part of your body than for your whole body to be thrown into hell. And if your right hand causes you to sin, cut it off and throw it away. It is better for you to lose one part of your body than for your whole body to go into hell. (Matthew 5:27-30, NIV)

The "Battle of Lust" for the heart of America became apparent in July 1976. Presidential candidate Jimmy Carter stood on the front steps of his home in Plains, Georgia and confronted the world with 4,000 years of Judeo-Christian morality as he confessed his struggle with lust to reporters: "I have looked on a lot of women with lust. I've committed adultery in my heart many times. This is something that I recognize offends God. . . . I have done it, yet I know God forgives me when I confess it to Him." This simple confession was ridiculed in headlines around the world, provoking millions to snicker and parody what was commonly perceived as antiquated puritanical notions.

Carter's admission was no less controversial in the Christian community. Christians responded with shock and surprise. Some expressed that the candidate lacked propriety—one is not supposed to talk about these things. Others felt that he had embarrassed his family and friends, hurt his image and jeopardized his presidential hopes. Some responded with pastoral advice regarding disciplines and prayers that would remove his struggle for all time. Still others simply exhorted him to have more faith.

Since 1976, on that humid summer day in Georgia, the smoke has cleared and we can see that the battle is over—lust has conquered American culture. Its mastery over our society is evident everywhere. Income from pornography has dramatically increased each of the last twenty years. Archibald Hart cites ninety-four percent of men raised in religious homes and ninety-eight percent of men raised in "secular" homes have been exposed to pornographic materials. The tragedy is that ninety-eight percent of all men polled acknowledge the destructive impact of pornography and lust, yet most feel powerless to address it.

Yet there is still reason to hope, however, because Jesus declares war on the secular god of lust despite society's continued denial concerning its destructive impact. This is the good news of the gospel: Jesus came to save us from our sin. His gospel is strategic. It attacks the root so that lives may be free from the tyranny of sin's brokenness. The same cross that saves us from the condemnation of sin also possesses the ability to rescue us from the power of sin. The key is that you must recognize and despise lust for what it is—sin!

Followers of Jesus Christ must not confuse what is "normal" with what is "acceptable," as the world around us does. While a society may attempt to engineer its values, God establishes our virtues and He has spoken out against lust. Why? Because it disorders and disorients the heart by causing it to crave what it cannot have. This uncontrolled sexual preoccupation will chisel away at your integrity and over time it will numb your ability to feel and experience intimacy. The other sex becomes an object, imaginations become voyeuristic and sexual fulfillment rather than faithfulness become our ambition in life.

Here are five practical steps for defeating lust in your life:

1. Pull out and destroy any pornographic material in your possession (this would include movies that contain explicit sexuality).

2. Stop feeding your fantasies. Deliberately distract your thoughts with other ideas or activities.
3. Be accountable to your spouse or another friend. Join a mentoring group or Bible study with members of the same sex.
4. Seek out healing prayer and/or find a Christian counselor. Do not underestimate the power of God to deliver you, nor the practical assistance a skilled counselor can offer you.
5. Finally, pray and receive God's grace. Remember "There is now no condemnation for those who are in Christ Jesus. For the law of the Spirit of life in Christ Jesus has set you free from the law of sin and of death" (Romans 8:1-2).

Until next week . . .

Integrity Values Repentance

The LORD sent Nathan to David. When he came to him, he said, "There were two men in a certain town, one rich and the other poor. The rich man had a very large number of sheep and cattle, but the poor man had nothing except one little ewe lamb he had bought. He raised it, and it grew up with him and his children. It shared his food, drank from his cup and even slept in his arms. It was like a daughter to him.

Now a traveler came to the rich man, but the rich man refrained from taking one of his own sheep or cattle to prepare a meal for the traveler who had come to him. Instead, he took the ewe lamb that belonged to the poor man and prepared it for the one who had come to him.

David burned with anger against the man and said to Nathan, "As surely as the LORD lives, the man who did this deserves to die! He must pay for that lamb four times over, because he did such a thing and had no pity."

> *Then Nathan said to David, "You are the man! This is what the LORD, the God of Israel says. . . . You struck down Uriah the Hittite with the sword and took his wife to be your own. You killed him with the sword of the Ammonites. Now, therefore, the sword will never depart from your house, because you despised me and took the wife of Uriah the Hittite to be your own. . . ."*
>
> *Then David said to Nathan, "I have sinned against the LORD." (2 Samuel 12:1-13, NIV)*

Kenneth Starr, special prosecutor who investigated President Clinton's moral and ethical conduct was not the first public official to expose secret sin in the private life of a national leader. Such was the role of the prophets in biblical times. Perhaps the most notorious example is Nathan's confrontation of David—Israel's beloved King. David was a leader's leader; he was also a Renaissance man. He was deeply spiritual, a soldier, philosopher, poet, musician, songwriter, husband, father and king. He was courageous, compassionate, a man of strategic vision. Yet he was clearly in touch with the joys and sorrows that were common to all people regardless of their power, wealth or status. He was uniquely endowed by God, a man for all seasons and a charismatic personality. Under his leadership the country flourished and expanded. Israel's borders were secure and her economy was strong.

Lamentably for David (and for his country), he also was a man who abused the powers of his office to indulge his sexual fantasies.

David's dalliance with Bathsheba was a personal affair, but it was not private. It mattered greatly to God, who judges a man for who he is on the inside (see 1 Samuel 16:7). It mattered to God, who had established his throne and endowed him with the gifts and abilities that had propelled him to national prominence. It mattered to God, who knew that David was compounding his sin by making decisions that intentionally put others at risk (especially Uriah!) so that he could conceal his personal sin. It mattered to God, who realized that David could not govern with moral authority or with public confidence if this breach of faith (before God and people) was not exposed. So God revealed David's sin to Nathan, who was then dispatched to confront David publicly.

It is here that we must understand that the true test of David's character was not the reality of his sin exposed, but his response once he was confronted. Would David continue to stonewall his accuser? Would he hide behind the authority of his office? Or would he receive Nathan as God's chastisement and respond appropriately with repentance? Would he face the consequences of God's discipline—whatever that may be?

President Clinton is not the first national leader to suffer public humiliation by acknowledging his

sexual problems. However, anyone who has leadership responsibilities (national, corporate or family) would be well advised to follow David's
example rather than the President's. David's heart
reflected authentic contrition and personal conviction. He did not hide his sin any longer. He owned
it and he recognized that he had sinned against
God (2 Samuel 12:13). He did not make excuses
and try to curry sympathy and understanding. He
did not lash out against the messenger who exposed his sin. He did not ask to be let off the hook
of public scrutiny by appealing to misplaced notions of privacy. He did not deceive and selfishly
hide behind the public advocacy of friends and col-
leagues for seven months. David simply, straight-
forwardly and immediately accepted complete
responsibility as he confessed and threw himself
on the mercy of God.

I do not write these words to perpetuate the
shaming of a President—which has now become
fashionable from all sides of the political spectrum.
I simply wish to point out that there is a world of
difference between admission and confession, between regret and contrition. Authentic conviction
for sin consumes the person affected with shame,
profound sorrow, guilt, a recognition of personal
defilement and a hunger for healing mercy that
can be found only at the foot of the cross of Jesus.
True conviction has no energy reserve that will allow one to lash out at others, nor does it draw so-
lace in pointing out others who may be guilty of
the same sin.

The President's actions and reactions were indicative of a man whose ethical edge has worn dull through compromise and self-indulgence. May it stand, like David's encounter with Nathan, as a prophetic warning to any of us who are not proactively keeping our ethical edge sharp by the power of the Holy Spirit. It is a sure pitfall that awaits anyone who turns a deaf ear to God's call to live holy and blameless lives. Let us invite the Holy Spirit to bring conviction as we examine our own lives rather than mock and deride the sins of others. We must be on our ethical guard lest we become so casual and comfortable that we too lose our ability to recognize our own temptations and perceive the power of sin still ruling in our own lives.

Until next week . . .

PART SEVEN

Committed

Husbands and wives who are eighty-five percent faithful to their spouse are not faithful at all. There is no such thing as part-time loyalty to Jesus Christ. It is all or nothing.

Are You Prepared?

ollowing Jesus makes life adventurous. When you follow Jesus you commit yourself, without reservation, to the most perfect, brilliant and exciting Person the world has ever seen. You will find no monotony in Him. Following Jesus will not make you boring or dull. He will make you holy—and that is a very different thing altogether. Biblical holiness is very attractive and very costly too. I think we draw back because we are afraid of the cost.

Let no one deceive you—it is undeniably costly to follow Jesus Christ. Everything about Jesus that we long to emulate and see evident in our own lives will not be realized through mediocrity and lukewarm commitment. He made this abundantly plain on many occasions. God offers His all to us all. But He wants all of us in return. Jesus outlined very clearly what it costs to follow Him:

> Large crowds were traveling with Jesus, and turning to them he said, "If anyone comes to me and does not hate his father

and mother, his wife and children, his brothers and sisters—yes, even his own life—he cannot be my disciple. And anyone who does not carry his cross and follow me cannot be my disciple.

"Suppose one of you wants to build a tower. Will he not first sit down and estimate the cost to see if he has enough money to complete it? For if he lays the foundation and is not able to finish it, everyone who sees it will ridicule him, saying, 'This fellow began to build and was not able to finish.'

"Or suppose a king is about to go to war against another king. Will he not first sit down and consider whether he is able with ten thousand men to oppose the one coming against him with twenty thousand? If he is not able, he will send a delegation while the other is still a long way off and will ask for terms of peace. In the same way, any of you who does not give up everything he has cannot be my disciple." (Luke 14:25-33, NIV)

There are five questions Jesus asks those who desire to follow Him:

1. *Are you prepared to put me first?* (14:26). Jesus has to come before parents and lovers and every other commitment. He demands our total obedience. He must come first in our

lives—not that there can ever be a true second behind Him. Jesus *is* our life. Only in Him do we have life, family and friendship. He must be the *Lord* Jesus Christ to anyone who would follow Him. Are you ready for this?

2. *Are you prepared to carry your cross?* (14:27). The cross was a very public event. Are you willing to "go public" as His follower? You will be laughed at, mocked and at times excluded. At other times you may find your cross heavy, painful and crushing. Contrary to popular understanding, carrying your cross has nothing to do with our worldly inconveniences and trials or our health. Carrying your cross is to publicly, without guile or self-advancement, follow the Lord wherever He will lead you. Are you ready for this?

3. *Are you prepared to keep going?* (14:28). Don't be like the project manager who hadn't figured out what it would cost him to complete his job. Jesus never asked anyone for a hasty commitment. He wants your lifelong allegiance. He is not looking for a simple decision. He wants disciples. Are you ready for this?

4. *Are you prepared for a struggle?* (14:31). Jesus likened discipleship to going to war. This means that you will enlist with Christ against the forces of evil in yourself and society. It is a call to integrity, courage and even unpopularity at times, as you declare war on the greed, lust, selfishness and fear within you and the

world around you. We will not finish the war in our lifetime but we can share in His progressive victory. Are you ready for this?

5. *Are you prepared to be in the minority?* (14:31-32). We all like to be part of the crowd. Our choices in fashion, fad and fun all reflect this natural human instinct to run with the crowd. Yet Jesus likened our discipleship to a leader who must figure out how to wage war with smaller resources. Christians are always in a minority because so many have not yet come to Him. Are you ready for this?

Until next week . . .

Faith without Commitment Is NO Faith at All

I do not trust in my bow,
  my sword does not bring me victory;
but you give us victory over our enemies,
  you put our adversaries to shame.
In God we make our boast all day. . . .
              (Psalm 44:6-8, NIV)

But this happened that we might not rely
on ourselves but on God, who raises the
dead. (2 Corinthians 1:9, NIV)

ociologists have long puzzled over surveys that suggest the United State is the most religious nation in the advanced, industrialized West. More than ninety percent of Americans, when asked, profess a belief in God. More than half say they pray at least once a day and more than forty percent claim to attend worship services in any given week. All this in a society that is overtly—even aggressively—secular, ethically relative and sexually permissive.

In the colonial era, many more citizens actually attended church than qualified for membership. Today, it appears, many more Americans claim regular church attendance than actually show up for worship. For example, The Gallup Organization reported that forty-five percent of American Protestants and fifty-one percent of American Roman Catholics attend services weekly in the 1990s—figures that are amazingly consistent with those of the last three decades. But according to a study published in the December 1993 issue of *American Sociological Review*, half the people who tell pollsters that they spend Sundays in church are not telling the truth. A team of sociologists headed by C. Kirk Hadaway of the United Church of Christ find that only twenty percent of Protestants and twenty-eight percent of Catholics show up on Sundays. Their figures are based on actual head counts in selected churches that they compared with surveys of the same communities. The explanation, says team member Mark Chaves of Notre Dame, is that "most people believe voting or going to church is a good thing to do and when surveyed often say they did vote or go to church even when they didn't."

Using an in-depth random survey of 4,001 Americans, the team has reconfigured the puzzle of American religion along the following lines: nearly a third of Americans eighteen and older are totally secular in outlook. This includes seven-and-a-half percent who describe themselves as atheists or agnostics along with twenty-two-and-a-half percent who exhibit what Green calls "only trace elements" of religion in their lives. According to their calculations, an additional twenty-two percent are barely or nominally religious. In short, they find that only nineteen percent of adult Americans— about 36 million people—regularly practice their religion. In other words, more than half of the American population claims a "religion" that *does not affect its attitudes or behavior.*

It is not enough to merely believe. True faith involves a personal commitment—

to believe,
to obey and
to do the work of Jesus.

True faith understands that commitments that cost us nothing are worth exactly what they cost us—nothing! True faith will truly change our lives and impact others.

Where do you really place your trust? As followers of Jesus Christ, we know the right answer in theory: "We trust in God!" But in practice, do we? When facing troubles, do we look to God for His way through, or do we manipulate things with using our wisdom and skill? When wanting guidance, do we wait until the Lord makes His will clear, or do we ask Him to bless our decisions? When deciding on direction, do we only consult those who are likely to agree with us? When tested, do we confidently look to God, or do we become fearful, negative, defeatist and/or preoccupied with our own weaknesses and limitations?

A.W. Tozer writes, "Many of us Christians have become extremely skillful in arranging our lives so as to admit the truth of Christianity without being embarrassed by its implications. . . . We boast in the Lord but watch carefully that we never get caught depending on Him."[9] Challenges and trials possess a clarity which easier, more predictable times do not. Turbulent times and trying circumstances remind us that there are ultimately two options for the follower of Jesus Christ—true faith or total collapse. Either He is Lord of all or He is not Lord at all.

The person who places his full trust in the Lord will quickly discover a wellspring of life that will not disappoint him or leave him weak, defenseless or ashamed (see John 7:38; Romans 5:1-5).

Are there people and circumstances that you have not placed in God's hands? If so, take a moment now to pray, "Lord Jesus, teach me to place my full trust in You. I trust You for . . ."

Until next week . . .

A Singular Passion

You have forsaken your first love. (Revelation 2:4, NIV)

Fix your thoughts on Jesus. (Hebrews 3:1, NIV)

The correspondence within the New Testament contains a distinctive focus and a singular challenge. The distinctive focus is the uniqueness and supremacy of Jesus Christ. The singular challenge is that believers in Jesus Christ should live like believers.

The book of Hebrews was written to Christians who were beset by difficult circumstances and besieged by impending tribulation. This letter was sent to encourage those tempted by their circumstances to give up their faith and abandon the distinctives of a Christian lifestyle. The central message of the letter is simple: "There is no one like Jesus . . . therefore, hold fast to Him."

The Father invites us to cling to Him who is: God's last word . . .

the Heir of all things . . .
    the creator of the universe . . .
        the reflection of God's glory . . .
    the great High Priest . . .
the supreme and final atonement for sin and the great Pastor who understands us completely.

Therefore, live like followers of Jesus and *hold fast to Him!*

Thirty-five years later, after the resurrection, the apostle John is inspired by Jesus Himself to write a letter to Christians in Ephesus who are facing turbulent times due to the apostasy of the city around them (Revelation 2). They strove to uphold God's truth and righteousness amidst a culture that had lost its moral and theological compass. Nevertheless, their passion for Jesus was in jeopardy and they were exhorted to return to their first love.

Followers of Jesus Christ, pay attention: There is one thing and one thing only that God is looking for—an abiding and lifelong passion for Jesus Christ. In God's eyes there are no excuses. War, persecution, success, illness, family strife, personal "woundedness," ministry and/or laboring for national righteousness are inadequate reasons for allowing our hearts to wane in our affection for Jesus Christ. God is responsible for your salvation. You are responsible to maintain your passion, love and affection for Jesus.

It is so easy to be taken up with other things, even Christian things, but nothing is more important than Jesus. We need to keep our first love for Him kindled, vibrant and responsive. After fourteen years of suffering under the communist regime of Romania, pastor Richard Wurmbrand wrote, "There exists only one method of resisting brain-washing and that is heart-washing. If the heart is cleansed by the love of Jesus, if the heart loves Him, you can resist all tortures" or successes or cultural shifts.

How do we maintain our first love? Indeed, some of us may need to ask a more painful question first: Has Jesus Christ ever been my first love?

Revelation 2:5 shows us the way: We must always be ready to "Repent and do the things you did at first" (NIV). Repenting means turning away from and confessing anything wrong in our lives, including a waning love for Jesus. What sort of things did the Ephesian Christians do at first?

* They came to the cross—is there ever a time when you do not need to call on God's grace?
* They were filled with the Spirit—is there ever a time when you don't need the Holy Spirit flooding your heart with the love of God or you?
* They gave serious attention to God's Word—is there ever a time when you don't need the clear, challenging and com-

pelling revelation of Scripture to encourage, teach, remind and discipline you?
☙ They burned their books on the occult and
got rid of anything that displeased Him—
is there ever a time when God is not calling you to take concrete action that expresses your total commitment to Him?

What did the Ephesians do? They put Him
first! Do you think that God expects us to do anything less?

Until next week . . .

Committed to Serve, Not Rule

Let a man regard us in this manner, as servants of Christ and stewards of the mysteries of God. In this case, moreover, it is required of stewards that one be found trustworthy. . . . Now these things, brethren, I have figuratively applied to myself and Apollos for your sakes, so that in us you may learn not to exceed what is written, so that no one of you will become arrogant in behalf of one against the other. For who regards you as superior? What do you have that you did not receive? And if you did receive it, why do you boast as if you had not received it? (1 Corinthians 4:1-2, 6-7)

Packed away in Paul's Corinthian correspondence is a very significant verse addressed to Christians who want to live as kings rather than surrender as servants. Like a two-edged sword, this verse possesses both a prophetic edge and a pastoral edge. Its prophetic edge threatens to lay bare our pride. Its pastoral edge reflects a devoted heart that is willing to challenge people to avoid unscriptural conduct. This verse (1 Corinthians 4:7) contains three simple questions that a child of God will want to pay special attention to:

1. *Who regards you as superior?* The Corinthian fellowship was a "legend in their own minds." They considered themselves too sophisticated for the simple, standard and mundane message that Paul preached. They were ready for more:

> Paul was flat . . .
>   they wanted flair;
> Paul was predictable . . .
>   they wanted astonishment;
> Paul was contrite . . .
>   they wanted extravagance;
> Paul preached the cross . . .
>   they wanted a crown;
> Paul called them servants . . .
>   they wanted to be lords.

The Corinthians were ecclesiastical narcissists. They considered themselves beyond the elementary teachings of the gospel. From their perspective they were already reigning with Jesus, richly endowed and superior to those weaker congregations that needed to dwell on the cross. They perceived themselves as elite leaders for a new age.

Paul responds to this by using two words to describe how a Christian leader should perceive himself—a servant and a steward. The first word carries with it the sense of personal answerability to Christ in whose service the person is engaged. The second word refers to the strategic activity of the crucial servant in a household. The steward's role was to transfer the resources of the owner to the members of his household according to their needs. Paul was warning the Corinthians that Christians must be careful not to confuse their leadership for lordship. We can aspire to be stewards and servants—nothing greater.

2. *What do you have that you did not receive?* Paul perceives that life, despite its ups and downs, is a gift from God Who lavishes upon us

> His Son, His Spirit and His Word;
> His love, His grace and His Church;
> talents, ability, insights, friendships
> and opportunities.

God does *not* help those who help themselves because there is no one who is so self-sufficient as to be able to "help himself" to these things! Reach out to grasp and you will find them fleeting. Reach out to receive and you will find your hands full.

The irony in all this is that eventually the Christian who wants to be "king" will never attain the quality of life that the steward/servant

will come to enjoy. Christian "lords" are con-
signed to struggle with

- *insecurity* (what if someone is better than
  me?);
- *scarcity* (what if I don't get enough?);
- *authority* (what if no one listens to me?);
- *serenity* (how can I be content when there
  is still so much to do?); and
- *authenticity* (how can I ever reveal what I
  am feeling or thinking?).

God's steward, on the other hand, will enjoy a
life that is

- *secure,* because his leadership rests in his
  calling in Christ and not in his superior
  abilities. God will equip him with everything he needs to succeed.
- *full,* because God provides out of His
  abundance. There are no competitive or
  diminishing resources with Him.
- *confident,* because his authority and ability is rooted in Jesus and not in the latest
  leadership technique.
- *peaceful,* because he can know God's pleasure and blessing as He prayerfully pur-
  sues his call and work.
- *truthful,* because there is nothing to hide or
  keep secret. The steward does not use or
  manipulate people for selfish purposes. Nor
  is his position predicated on proprietary or

confidential information. Secrets are unnecessary.

3. *Why do you boast as if you had not received it?*
   There is nothing that obscures the beauty,
   grace and power of Jesus Christ more than
   Christians who insist on promoting themselves. Can the Holy Spirit

   - fill those who are already full of them-
     selves?
   - equip those who already feel they know it
     all?
   - empower those who already feel able?
   - instruct those who feel they have moved
     beyond their Teacher?

Furthermore, there can be no true Church where
"lords" reside for two simple reasons. First, in the
Church there is only one Lord—all the rest are servants. Second, there can be no true fellowship of
"lords," for each will be distracted by his need to
preserve and extend his own kingdom. Competi-
tion is the hallmark of lords, while surrender, sacrifice and service distinguish a fellowship of
stewards.

Let these three questions penned by a well-
seasoned soul challenge you to reconsider your
own perspective, priorities and purpose.

Until next week . . .

Committed to Seeing God's Work in Your Work

> In a large house there are articles not only of gold and silver, but also of wood and clay; some are for noble purposes and some for ignoble. If a man cleanses himself from the latter, he will be an instrument for noble purposes, made holy, useful to the Master and prepared to do any good work. (2 Timothy 2:20-21, NIV)

f you are a follower of Jesus Christ who hungers to see His glory, power and love tangibly manifest in our world today, then let me declare to you an amazing truth: God has prepared you to do "any good work" *at work*!

God has chosen you for noble purposes. You can make choices today that will honor God where you work. Your vocation is the location of your witness for Christ—this is your noble purpose for which He has placed you in your current job. You are there for reasons more strategic than merely drawing a paycheck. He has a people to bless through you and kingdom ground to gain through you. Silence, indifference, neutrality, busyness and timidity cannot achieve what God has placed you there to accomplish. He has placed you there to be in relationship with others so that they may have the opportunity to see the surpassing greatness of our God through you. Take a moment right now and pray this simple prayer:

> *My God and Father, please give me a fresh sense of Your purposes for me here at work. Fill me afresh with Your Holy Spirit that I might behold the strategic opportunities You have for me here. Free me from distractions and the cares of this world, which I allow to dull my vision for Your work here. Free me, fill me and use me here. Amen.*

Jesus—not your work—is the Lord of your life. You must not misplace His authority over you by transferring it to others in order to justify dishonorable actions. We must not compromise the Lordship of Jesus Christ by blind obedience to others. Jesus calls us to submit, serve and love those who have authority over us. However, nowhere does He call us to engage in unrighteous behavior merely because we are asked by someone in authority. The Lordship of Jesus mandates that every follower of Jesus Christ keep his ethical edge sharp. Every ethical compromise is a public, albeit temporary, renunciation of our confession of His

Lordship. Either Jesus Christ is Lord of all or He is not Lord at all. Your job is the public arena where you are called to bring the reality of God's presence and the confession of His Lordship. Take a moment and pray this simple prayer:

> *Jesus, You are Lord over my life. You are Lord over my home, my friendships, my finances, my time and my work. All that I have, all that I am and all that I hope to be belongs to You. Your love and Your Lordship encompass every area of my life—including my work. I pray that You will convict me of anything or anyone that I am holding back from You or placing before You. Amen.*

You are called to be an overcomer. You are free to love the world as God loves the world. You are not bound by the same rules as the non-Christian. You are liberated to serve, love and care for others at work, whether they are CEOs or peons. You are free to serve everyone in the same manner as Jesus. You are free to overcome ethnic division by building friendships. You are free to restore hope to those who are disillusioned and despairing. You are free to solicit prayer requests for the needs of those around you. You have the authority to renounce evil when you see its vile head rise up at work. You are free to respect all manner of people without regard for status, gender, appearance, ethnicity or wealth. You are free from power games, schemes and the rat race because your security, hope and future lie in the sovereign purposes of Jesus Christ. You cannot lose a job He wants you to keep! You cannot keep a job He wants you to leave! Take a moment to pray:

> *Lord, You have called me to be an overcomer here at work. I confess that I frequently cave in rather than rise above my circumstances. Teach me Your ways, Lord. Renew a right spirit within me. Create in me the same attitude that was in Jesus. Help me not to love and seize power but to see my life as an offering to You and as an opportunity to serve, lead and love in the manner of Jesus. Amen.*

It is God's intention to prepare you for any and every good work, wherever you work, so that in all your work Jesus Christ may be honored.

Until next week . . .

PART EIGHT

Empowered

Picture this: a photo of tornado damage in a small Texas town. There in the middle of the picture is a telephone pole that has been pierced through by a thin branch of wheat . . .

Consider this: The natural limitations of what are meaningless when accompanied by the power of a tornado.

Remember this: Jesus said that the Holy Spirit is like the wind.

Be Strong in God's Power

> My message and my preaching were
> not with wise and persuasive words,
> but with a demonstration of the Spirit's
> power, so that your faith might not rest
> on men's wisdom, but on God's power.
> (1 Corinthians 2:4-5, NIV)

> Finally, be strong in the Lord and in
> his mighty power. (Ephesians 6:10, NIV)

"Words! Words! I'm sick of words! Show me!" This is the exasperating cry of Eliza Doolittle to Professor Henry Higgins in the classic musical, *My Fair Lady*. It is also the cry of everyone who has watched his or her Christian life decay and grow devoid of God's power. Faith becomes the mere affirmation of orthodox doctrine and/or an endless series of self-help steps. Powerless Christian faith substitutes fatigue for vitality, victim for overcomer and a whisper for a shout!

169

We desperately need to appropriate God's power to live the life that reflects His destiny and not our own futility or striving. I am not calling for a life of triumphalistic lunacy but a life where we are conscious of the Lord's life-giving endowment through the person and power of the Holy Spirit. This requires nothing more (and nothing less) than your trust.

First, you must have a settled and firm trust that the Lord is almighty in power—this is absolutely essential. Second, you must trust that this almighty power of God is engaged on your behalf. Third, you must trust in His mighty power by leaning on Him when you face every trial and temptation. Do you know that God will reach forth with His power just as a loving father reaches out with his hand to steady the walk of his uncertain toddler?

This week, let me suggest to you three reasons why you can trust yourself to God's power.

1. *His past record.* Throughout history God proves the sufficiency of His power, yet it is not always easy for His children to believe that He is almighty. Mary and Martha shared their doubts with Jesus when one exclaimed, "If You had been here, my brother would not have died" and the other said, "Lord, by this time there will be a stench, for he has been dead four days" (John 11:32, 39). Both were godly women but one expressed her doubts as to place—"if you had been here." The other limited His power to time—"by now his body stinks." Yet neither

time nor place limits the power of the Lord. Jesus is never too late. The grave will always give up its dead at His command. The Scriptures are a résumé of God's faithfulness—what He has done for others in the past He can do for you in the present.

2. *Your present circumstances.* The true challenges of life will always stretch beyond the limits of your ingenuity and fortitude. All Christians, whether they know it or not, are engaged in spiritual conflict. The world, the flesh and the devil conspire together to steadily hack away at your faith and your resolve. Together they want to break you so you will throw away the pitcher of faith that first day the well appears dry. But take notice! These struggles coupled with your powerlessness are, in fact, opportunities for you to be to be strong in the Lord and in His mighty power. If you could succeed alone there would be no opportunity to trust.

3. *God's eternal desire.* It has ever been and always will be the Father's desire that we trust only in Him. We may be wise, merciful and mighty according to human standards but He alone is all-wise, all-merciful and all-mighty. God's timely interventions reflect His eternal desire and confirm that you can trust that His almighty power is engaged for your defense.

Take a moment right now to consider an area of your life where you want to see God's power prevail. Confess your weakness . . . surrender yourself to Him and His timing . . . and ask the Father to fill you afresh with the power of the Holy Spirit.

Next week we will discuss the four biblical truths which secure us God's power.

Until next week . . .

The Promise of Power

*In the same way God, desiring even
more to show to the heirs of the promise the unchangeableness of His purpose, interposed with an oath, so that
by two unchangeable things in which it
is impossible for God to lie, we who
have taken refuge would have strong
encouragement to take hold of the hope
set before us. (Hebrews 6:17-18)*

Chutzpah: Yiddish word implying shame-
less audacity, impudence, presumptuous
nerve. *Chutzpah* breaches all social convention and tact to ask for that which it is deemed
inappropriate to receive or absurd to expect.
Parrhesia: New Testament Greek word implying
boldness, trust, certainty, conquest, effective
power and expectation. *Parrhesia* asks for and expects that which social convention considers impossible if not implausible.

Question: When a Christian asks God for power,
is it *chutzpah* or is it *parrhesia*?

Answer: That depends on God! Has He given us certain signs that He has bound Himself to us so that we might approach Him with boldness and expect His power? Here are four truths clearly presented in Scripture that testify that our God has engaged His power on our behalf.

1. *God's kinship with His saints.* God's relationship with us assures His power on our behalf. A Christian is His own dear child by adoption through Jesus Christ. A mother sitting in her house hears a sudden cry outside and, knowing the voice, says at once, "That is my child!" She drops everything at once and runs to him. God responds with a mother's heart to the cries of her children. Even the silly hen dashes about to gather her brood under her wing when trouble appears. How much more will God, who is the designer of such inclinations in His creatures, stir up His whole strength to defend you?

2. *God's dear love for His saints.* God's love for His saints sets His power in motion. He who has God's heart will not lack for God's arm. When a man comes to faith in Jesus Christ, then God's eternal purpose and counsel concerning him—whom He chose in Christ before the foundation of the world—is brought to fruition. Can you imagine, for a moment, the love that God has for the child he has carried so long in the womb of His sovereign purpose? If God delighted in His plan before He spoke the world into life,

how much greater is His delight when He witnesses the fruit of His labor—a man twice-born in Jesus! God will surely raise up all the power He has on that believer's behalf rather than have His glory plundered by the adversary's devices. God demonstrated to us how much we are worth by the price He paid. He who spent His Son's life to rescue you will spend His own power to keep you.

3. *God's everlasting covenant.* God's covenant engages His mighty power because He freely chooses to obligate Himself to prove that He is trustworthy. Through the covenant He has established with us in Christ, He has bound Himself to use His power in our defense. He does not dole out His power like we feed crumbs to birds—to make a little go a long way. He promises to withhold nothing and instead gives all He has to each of His beloved.

4. *God's interceding Son.* Jesus Christ ascended to the right hand of God where He "reminds" our Father of His firm commitment to defend His beloved. (Note: This biblical imagery is intended to describe Jesus' ongoing ministry rather than portray a God who would otherwise remain callous to your circumstances.) We remain in God's heart and He will not forget us for a moment. Consider how He kept His promise to the apostles that they would not be left as orphans. His throne next to the Father was barely warm when the Holy Spirit was dispatched to His people. How could God

remain indifferent and aloof with His power when Jesus intercedes on your behalf without ceasing?

Powerless Christianity has never been a question of the availability of God's power for daily living. The true issue has been our willingness to live daily by God's power. God's power and sure defense are available to the man who comes and asks.

> Finally, be strong in the Lord and in his mighty power. Put on the full armor of God so that you can take your stand against the devil's schemes. (Ephesians 6:10-11, NIV)

Until next week . . .

God's Strength for Daily Living

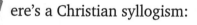

If God is for us, who can be against us? . . . Who will bring any charge against those whom God has chosen? . . . Who shall separate us from the love of Christ? (Romans 8:31, 33, 35, NIV)

Here's a Christian syllogism:

1. A Christian is one who has the omnipotent God in charge of his life.
2. No assault can overpower God and there is no force that can compel Him.
3. Therefore, a Christian can stop worrying about how to fight his daily battles because there is no one who can overpower God.

Nothing can penetrate the "front lines" of a Christian's life unless there is premature surrender on our part first. An attack against a Christian is not merely an attack against a person, but against the presence of God which fills the believer's life.

Has God's power grown weaker today or are our enemies stronger? Has progress given sin, death and the devil the leading edge? Certainly not! Never confuse sin's bravado for power. While evil may frighten and intimidate men, it is nothing but arrogant bluster before our Almighty God. The constant demonstrations of God's power on behalf of His saints stand in sharp relief to the impotent aid that Satan's counterfeits offer as an alternative.

Strengthen yourself in the knowledge that God's strong arm reaches down to you in love. With the same faith that persuades you that God exists, creates and saves, believe this too: His almighty power is your sure friend. You can put it to the test in the following circumstances:

1. *When you are weighed down by sin.* You can be certain that no sin is powerful enough to overpower God or to nullify His saving work in Jesus Christ. God, like any king, has always had the power to pardon anyone He chooses to. But our confidence does not rest upon His divine whim. The gospel declares that God has freely decided, within the counsel of His will, to establish a covenant to pardon. God has determined to drown your sins in His mercy, spend all He has and spare not His own rather than let it be said that His steadfast goodness can be overcome by our evil. When sin and Sa-

tan terrorize your soul, you can confidently proclaim, "If God is for me, who can prevail against God? Has He ever broken a promise?"

2. *When overpowered by temptation.* Our Father watches us carefully while we are in the valley of distress and conflict. Your cries bring Him running—although, in fact, He has never left you. It is the Lord and not a man who has declared, "Sin shall not be master over you" (Romans 6:14). While we may be weak and frail, our strength lies in the rock of God's faithfulness. All the Christian need do is to take shelter within its shade. However, what good will the shade of a mighty rock do us if we deliberately venture forth into the heat of temptation? Why should we be surprised when our faith grows so weak that we stumble and fall into sin?

3. *When overwhelmed by work and circumstances.* God knows the limits of your strength because His watchful eye is always upon you. When temptation causes you to stagger, He will pick you up, burden and all, and carry you to your God-appointed destination. Your first line of defense is not to wrestle but to rest in His promise: "And God is faithful; he will not let you be tempted beyond what you can bear. But when you are tempted, he will also provide a way out so that you can stand up under it" (1 Corinthians 10:13, NIV).

God is resolved to allow the weakest among us to move Him to action by the mere whisper (whimper?) of His name. The very sight of you in prayer will move His heart to mercy and carry a strong argument for His aid on your behalf.

Until next week . . .

Empowered Endurance

Do you not know that in a race all the runners run, but only one gets the prize? Run in such a way as to get the prize. (1 Corinthians 9:24, NIV)

Brothers, I do not consider myself yet to have taken hold of it. But one thing I do: Forgetting what is behind and straining toward what is ahead, I press on toward the goal to win the prize for which God has called me heavenward in Christ Jesus. (Philippians 3:13-14, NIV)

Failure is inevitable. It is not a question of "if"; it is simply a matter of "when." At the heart of the matter is our mistaken notion that the experience is an epitaph—a verdict that marks us for the remainder of our lives. It is almost as if Descartes' famous Enlightenment dictum, "I think, therefore I am," has mutated into an equally errant postulation, "I fail, therefore I am a failure." Setbacks, missed expectations, unrealistic goals, rejection, mistakes, ineffective programs/results, poor decisions, poor timing, etc.—this and more are realities of life. Yet, by God's grace, from them arise wisdom, focus, faith, resolve, character and hope.

Failure is inevitable. What we need is a Holy Spirit-inspired resiliency that empowers us to "press on toward the goal to win the prize for which God has called us heavenward in Christ Jesus." No one exemplifies this better than the sixteenth president of the United States, Abraham Lincoln:

1818	His mother died.
1831	Failed in business.
1832	Lost his job. Wanted to go to law school but couldn't get in.
1833	Borrowed money from a friend to begin business and by the end of the year he was bankrupt. He spent the next eleven years of his life paying off this debt.
1834	Ran for state legislature—won.
1835	Was engaged to be married; sweetheart died and his heart was broken.
1836	Had a total nervous breakdown and was in bed for six months.
1838	Sought to become Speaker of the state legislature—was defeated.
1840	Sought to become elector—was defeated.
1843	Ran for Congress—lost.

1846	Ran for Congress again—this time he won.
1848	Ran for reelection to Congress—lost.
1849	Sought the job of land officer in his home state—rejected.
1854	Ran for the U.S. Senate—lost.
1856	Sought the Vice-Presidential nomination at his party's national convention—he received less than 100 votes.
1858	Ran for U.S. Senate again—again he lost.
1860	Elected President of the United States![10]

Chuck Smith, the founder of the Calvary Chapel movement, never pastored a church larger than 175. For seventeen years he labored to see men and women come to Christ but with little success. Discouraged, he accepted a call to a small, nondescript congregation in Costa Mesa, California, where he pressed on, undeterred by what he thought were his past failures. Over 1,100 churches have since been planted around the world as a result of his ministry. . . .

Failure is not the arbiter of our future as much as it is the barometer of our present character and fortitude. Therefore . . .

Do not be discouraged . . .
   run the race
      by the power of God
         for the glory of God
           and run it to win!

The stumbles and defeats of today are of no account when seen through the lens of God's "tomorrow" for you. Yet from them God's grace will produce wisdom, focus, faith, resolve, character and a hope in Jesus that will not put us to shame.

Until next week . . .

PART NINE:

World-Changing

There is no way of foreseeing what may yet become part of history. But there now exist followers of Jesus whose impact can release tomorrow's history today.

A Person of Impact

But you, man of God, flee from all this, and pursue righteousness, godliness, faith, love, endurance and gentleness. Fight the good fight of the faith. Take hold of the eternal life to which you were called when you made your good confession in the presence of many witnesses. In the sight of God, who gives life to everything, and of Christ Jesus, who while testifying before Pontius Pilate made the good confession, I charge you to keep this command without spot or blame until the appearing of our Lord Jesus Christ. (1 Timothy 6:11-14, NIV)

People can be divided into three groups: those who make things happen, those who watch things happen and those who wonder what happened! Timothy, the subject of this Scripture passage, is charged by Paul to aspire to be in the first group. In other words, God intends him to be a man of impact.

Today there are three main reasons why our world needs followers of Jesus Christ who will make an impact.

First, our world is changing. By next year at this time there will be at least 125 million more people in the world than there are now. Who will lead them? Will our leaders develop or destroy them? Who or what will shape their understanding of truth, justice, morality and destiny?

Second, many in leadership positions have abdicated their responsibility—either intentionally or functionally. In the United States, a majority no longer consider character an essential ingredient of good leadership.

Third, people fear change! Change will occur whether there is effective leadership or not. Without positive leadership, change will bring deterioration and destruction rather than growth and improvement. Leadership crises occur because change will not wait for leadership. Society is not like a car parked in a driveway waiting for a driver. It is like an automobile careening down the freeway at seventy miles per hour. Without a driver, it will surely crash. If the driver is reckless or drunken, the results will be tragic. If the driver is misguided, the destination which the hearts of humanity yearn for will never be reached.

Every follower of Jesus Christ is called to be a person of impact. The Spirit of God forbids you to remain silent or passive while the world, the flesh and the devil plunder, blind and confound your "impact zone." Your "impact zone" includes yourself, your friends, family and coworkers. While the size and scope of this "impact zone" may vary from person to person, mark this: Your temperament neither accredits nor disqualifies you. It is your responsiveness to God's call and your readiness to do His will that certify you to be a person of impact.

A person of impact will deliberately exert special influence within his "impact zone" in order to move men, women, youth and children toward a destination established by God. To accomplish this,

- People of impact realize that vision is the foundation of their leadership. Vision is a revelation of the will of God for us. Spiritual vision doesn't simply fix what is wrong or broken—it redesigns.
- People of impact set goals of beneficial permanence that fulfill God's wishes and address people's real needs.
- People of impact recognize their responsibility to take initiative and not to remain passive. People of impact will take deliberate action in keeping with God's call, truth and mercy.
- People of impact understand their need to cultivate personal discipline and purity.

Neither the world nor the Church needs a coterie of elitists who talk love and compassion while isolating themselves from real people. People are not looking for a retinue of cliché-spouting, self-avowed "quick fix" magicians. The world is looking

for people of impact—only those who are committed to Jesus and compassionately concerned for
people will make a lasting difference.

Until next week...

Nothing Is Impossible for God

Ananias answered, "Lord, I have heard from many about this man, how much harm he did to Your saints at Jerusalem; and here he has authority from the chief priests to bind all who call on Your name." But the Lord said to him, "Go, for he is a chosen instrument of Mine, to bear My name before the Gentiles and kings and the sons of Israel." (Acts 9:13-15)

Ananias had a problem. God summoned him to share the message of the gospel with the rabbi Saul of Tarsus—the man we know as the apostle Paul. Yet for Ananias, there was not a more unlikely man to become a follower of Jesus Christ than Paul. Paul was an esteemed man with a passion, but he was also an opinionated, legalistic, zealous man who was so sure of what he believed that he was willing to see people killed who departed from his understanding of faith in God. Paul literally had a "take-no-prisoners" approach to his faith.

Ananias' problem is our problem too! We have many people in our circle of relationships that we have judged unlikely (impossible?) to ever respond positively to Jesus Christ. Yet those we consider unlikely, God may consider a "sure thing" because He knows the hearts of all.

Opportunities abound for sharing the truth of Jesus Christ. However, we only perceive these opportunities to the extent that we really want to. The crucial question is not, "God, will You give me a chance to speak about Jesus to others?" The true question is really, "Do I want to take the opportunities God is giving me to speak to others about Jesus?"

I remember being on study leave once and not wanting to speak to anyone about anything, but the Lord challenged me to the contrary! I said, "All right, Lord, I am willing to speak to anyone in this hotel about You if You guide me to someone." And He did! The next morning a man, who by all appearances had it made, joined me for breakfast. He had an exciting career, beautiful family, was physically fit, intelligent, good-looking. In short, he was a real leader-type. Soon the conversation came around to the usual question, "What do you do?"— usually a conversation killer when a non-Christian discovers I am a pastor! But not this time! He quickly confessed to me that he didn't know which way he was going in life, and what followed was a beautiful opportunity to share the gospel and tell of the love and purposeful presence of Jesus Christ in my life.

Many people are hungry for God, however self-confident or uninterested they may appear to be. Many times I have needed this reminder because appearances are deceptive. All people need Jesus! I discovered this truth anew that day.

Scripture clearly reveals that God has a vision for unlikely people—Abraham, Gideon, David, Peter and Paul, just to name a few! God desires us to have this same vision for the unlikely people that He wants to reach out through us. Take a moment right now and prayerfully consider people in your network of relationships that you disqualified as improbable, if not impossible. Some may be family members or even close friends. Some may be at work with you right now. Would you take a moment right now and ask God to give you His insight and compassion so that you may have

a rekindled faith,
a refreshed expectation,
a refocused vision and
a renewed passion

for the people that He may be placing in your heart and mind? Finally, ask God to use you in any manner He sees fit to share the life that is within you.

Until next week . . .

Never Underestimate Your Impact

When they saw the courage of Peter and John and realized that they were unschooled, ordinary men, they were astonished and they took note that these men had been with Jesus. (Acts 4:13, NIV)

The disciples had no special qualifications; they were neither theologically trained nor notably mystical. You don't have to be a specialist to be an active witness for Jesus. The only BA you need is "Born Again," followed by firsthand experience with the presence of Jesus in your life.

I have noticed that the witness of any Christian is more effective than the witness of a pastor. People expect a pastor to speak about Jesus—after all, we're paid to do it! People are far more impacted when their coworkers or friends talk about Him because this is unexpected (!) and because they are more approachable and relevant. Since you share many of the same commitments and interests, your friends or coworkers can easily relate with you.

You are surrounded by men and women whom Jesus wants to impact through you. I am convinced that no one else has the chance to reach them like you do. Why? Because you are a Christian—not by what you do (or refrain from!) but because Jesus Christ dwells in you by the power of the Holy Spirit. He desires to work through you to touch the hearts of other men and women. The marketplace is His mission field. It is the field to which He has called you as a full-time Christian minister so that He might do the extraordinary through you.

You are called to be what Jim Cymbala, pastor of the Brooklyn Tabernacle in New York, calls an "ordinary hero":

> . . . a man or woman who applied their strength and courageous action toward what God has promised. . . . These heroes did not just sit back, as many do today, saying, "Well, God promised, and I'm sure He will fulfill His word." They stepped up and took action to make the promise become a reality. They understood that God's work in the world is usually a joint project; He works with us as we yield ourselves to Him. . . . Similarly, the gospel of Jesus Christ will be planted today in hostile cities and terri-

tories and nations only by mighty men and women who dare to take risks. . . .

What we desperately need in our own time are not Christians full of cant and posturing, railing at the world's problems of secular humanism, New Age, or whatever. We need men and women who will step out to turn back today's slide toward godlessness. . . . When it comes to spiritual matters, you and I will never know our potential under God until we step out and take risks.[11]

Take a few moments right now and jot down the names of friends, neighbors or people at work whose Christian faith you are unsure of and then take a moment right now to pray for them.

You are a full-time Christian minister whose vocation is the strategic location where God has placed you for service and witness. May He give you favor, strength, love and patience as you serve Him there.

Until next week . . .

There Is Nothing Dull about Jesus

For we cannot stop speaking about what we have seen and heard. (Acts 4:20)

hristianity? No thanks—too dull for me." This is the impression from many non-Christians I meet who think that the Christian faith is boring, restrictive and divided. The average person does not expect celebration and robust enthusiasm in a Sunday worship service. In fact, a favorite observation among pundits is that people turn to cults because the Church in our society is popularly perceived as tedious and legalistic—emphasizing all of the "should-have-could-have-ought-to-dos-and-don'ts."

But make no mistake about it—dullness is not a necessary trademark of biblical Christianity. In the first-century world that witnessed the birth of the early Church, friend and foe alike had many descriptive words for Christianity. I can assure you that "dull" was not on the list! Today, around the world, people are discovering a fullness of life they had only dreamed of before meeting Jesus.

There is nothing dull about Jesus. Jesus is the most compelling personality in history. In His day some may have thought Him subversive, others radical and still others considered Him dangerous. The one word no one would have considered using was *dull*. More books have been written about Him, more music composed to honor Him and more art directed toward Him than any other figure in history. Go to nearly any country today and you will meet people who vividly describe their personal encounter with Him. In fact, no minute of the day passes without men, women, youth and children singing His praise and extolling His majesty. The sun never sets on the praises of His people.

There is nothing dull about His teaching. No boring dos and don'ts. No long sermons filled with empty and esoteric jargon. No theological abstractions or spiritual elitism. His teaching was memorable and powerful. Nearly all of His most revered teachings were spoken outdoors. Women and children, as well as men, were invited to listen—and listen they did! On one occasion over 5,000 gathered to listen to this teacher from Nazareth. He spoke about money, sex, power, forgiveness, anger, peace, apocalyptic futures, heaven, hell, marriage, divorce, lust and greed. His perspective was frequently revolutionary—but never dull!

There is nothing dull about the claims of Jesus. He claimed to teach the truth with the final authority of God Himself. He claimed to be able to forgive sins—something only God can do! He claimed that He would judge the world. He claimed that He was able to satisfy the deepest longing of the human heart. He claimed to be God's Son. He claimed the right to receive worship. C.S. Lewis says it best when he comments:

> The really foolish thing that people say about Him is that "I'm ready to accept Him as a great moral teacher, but I don't accept His claim to be God." A man who is merely a man and said the sort of things Jesus said would not be a great moral teacher. He would either be a lunatic—on a level with a man who says he is a poached egg—or else He would be the devil of hell. You must make your choice. Either this man was and is the Son of God: or else a madman or something worse.[12]

There is nothing dull about His challenge. Jesus did not send people away to write books or sequester themselves in monasteries, require celibacy or offer good advice. He did not mince words when He said: "Come to me," "Follow me," "Sell all you have," "Lay down your life for me," or "Why do you call me Lord, Lord, and not do what I tell you?" He challenged His followers to pay their taxes, to love their enemies, to bless their oppressors, to become as servants, to rejoice in their sufferings, to love one another as He had loved them and to take up their own cross and follow Him. Dietrich Bonhoeffer summarized Christ's challenge this way: "When Christ calls a man, He bids him come and die."

🕰 🕰 🕰 🕰 🕰

Anyone who finds Him dull has not found Him. That person may have seized the counterfeit clone that religion can create, but he does not know Jesus! The Jesus I know will love you, surprise you, convict you, empower you, send you, free you, purify you, fill you, lead you, discipline you, forgive you, save you, deliver you and bless you. There is no boredom in His presence. Even silence and stillness become alive with His fullness.

No, there is nothing dull about Jesus. . . . My prayer is that our life and witness, in Christ, will be a living repudiation of this lie.

Until next week . . .

A Love That Wins Hearts

This is how God showed his love among us: He sent his one and only Son into the world that we might live through him. This is love: not that we loved God, but that he loved us and sent his Son as an atoning sacrifice for our sins. Dear friends, since God so loved us, we also ought to love one another. No one has ever seen God; but if we love one another, God lives in us and his love is made complete in us. (1 John 4:9-12, NIV)

ivine revelation and human revolutions share one thing in common: Both require new vocabularies to describe their worldview, their understanding of the future and their ethic. New words are created and old words are redefined. Such is the case concerning the Christian understanding of love. While other religions and ideologies may share certain Christian beliefs (i.e., there is only one God) and behavior (i.e., giving to the poor), one factor that is distinctive and unique about Christianity is love— the love of God made real in our hearts and relationships by the Holy Spirit. This love is so different from other understandings or expressions found elsewhere in the world that the New Testament writers had to redefine a new Greek word to articulate it. This word is found nowhere else in other writings of that period.

The Greeks knew all about sexual love, about natural family affection, about the special bond between husband and wife, the strong cord of friendship and a sense of wonderment before the gods or nature. Their philosophers, poets, artists and playwrights eloquently brought these reflections to life. Nevertheless, the Christian word for love that appears 250 times in the New Testament isn't found in any of their literature or art. In nearly every reference in the New Testament this word is used to describe God's relationship with man. This word describes the love of God

> that is supremely concerned for
>   the highest good of humanity;
> that gives and gives and gives
>   without thought of reciprocity;
> that is willing to lay down its life
>   for the benefit of others;
> that stands ready to forgive anyone
>   for anything;
> a love that initiates, calls, provides,
>   strengthens, heals and sets people free.

This love is exemplified in the person and work of Jesus Christ—"But God demonstrates His own love toward us, in that while we were yet sinners, Christ died for us" (Romans 5:8).

This love can also be witnessed among Christians when the Holy Spirit is working in our midst. I have had the opportunity to talk with many people from other worldviews who have come to faith in Jesus Christ. Among these people have been atheists, people from other faiths, communists, ex-Nazis, the rich, the poor, children, teens, adults, senior citizens and people from every continent. The one thing that convinced them of the truth about Jesus and the reality of God was the quality of love they found among Christians. I also recognize, with sadness, that the opposite is also true. Many today remain unconvinced about the spiritual realities Christians bear witness to simply because they do not see this love which should always be the outstanding mark of the Church. Gandhi once said to a Christian leader in India, "In that day when we see Jesus Christ living out His love in you, on that day we Hindus will flock to your Christ."

Until next week . . .

PART TEN

Victorious

Victorius is a state of mind rather than a success achieved. It is not contingent upon circumstances but is established upon God's promises and presence. Therefore, defeat and failure are not its biggest threat. . . . Ego is.

That Was Then . . . This Is Now

Now it came about when Joshua was by Jericho, that he lifted up his eyes and looked, and behold, a man was standing opposite him with his sword drawn in his hand, and Joshua went to him and said to him, "Are you for us or for our adversaries?" And he said, "No; rather I indeed come now as captain of the host of the LORD." And Joshua fell on his face to the earth, and bowed down, and said to him, "What has my lord to say to his servant?" The captain of the LORD's host said to Joshua, "Remove your sandals from your feet, for the place where you are standing is holy." And Joshua did so. (Joshua 5:13-15)

That was then . . . this is now.

Then Joshua was forty years younger . . .
  Then Moses was in charge . . .
    Then God seemed to work miracles daily . . .
      Then there was so much momentum, but . . .
Then common sense supplanted faith . . .

Then the people abandoned
      their future to fear . . .
            Then the nation wandered for forty years . . .
            Then Joshua witnessed the death
                  of his generation . . .

But that was then and this is now . . .

Now Joshua is forty years older . . .
      Now Jericho's walls are no smaller . . .
            Now Jericho's streets are no less populated . . .
                  Now Jericho's might has not diminished . . .

Now Joshua is forty years older . . .
      Now he stands before a fortified city . . .
            Now he has no battle plans . . .
                  Now the risks of defeat are real . . .

Now Joshua is forty years older—and the underdog.
      Now his troops are young and inexperienced . . .
            Now he does not hold a strategic position . . .
                  Now he lacks the element of surprise . . .
                  Now he needs a miracle . . .

That was then . . . this is now.

Then it was the eve of a great battle . . .
      Then, behold! A man standing opposite him . . .
            Then the man's sword was drawn . . .
                  Then Joshua lifted up his eyes and looked . . .

Now Joshua is still forty years older . . .
      Now he is not the warrior he once was . . .
            Now Joshua is still a man of vision . . .
                  Now there is still hope . . .
                  Now Joshua still sees . . .

Jericho is not just a city to conquer . . .
   Jericho is not merely the enemy . . .
      Jericho is not simply an obstacle to overcome . . .
   Jericho is not a racial issue (Jew vs. Gentile) . . .
Jericho is not solely the execution of divine wrath . . .

Now Joshua is forty years older . . .
   Now Joshua is a man of vision and
      Now Joshua sees the truth . . .

Before Jericho falls,
   Joshua must bow . . .
Before Jericho is defeated,
   Joshua must surrender . . .

Loved ones, you stand at a threshold full of our Father's opportunities for you. What happened in the past must no longer influence your determination to possess the strategic present and future God has for you. Your greatest challenge this year will not be acquisitions, growth, change, loss, sorrow or age. Your greatest challenge will be to bow and fully surrender to the Lordship of Jesus Christ. This means surrendering to Him everything in your life you are withholding. Vision without surrender is thinly disguised vanity.

Joshua learned that God does not take sides, but calls us to His.

Until next week . . .

Defeating Intimidation (Part 1)

> *Now Jericho was tightly shut. . . . The LORD said to Joshua, "See, I have given Jericho into your hand. . . . You shall march around the city, all the men of war circling the city once. You shall do so for six days. Also seven priests shall carry seven trumpets of rams' horns before the ark; then on the seventh day you shall march around the city seven times, and the priests shall blow the trumpets. . . . When you hear the sound of the trumpet, all the people shall shout with a great shout; and the wall of the city will fall down flat." (Joshua 6:1-5)*

Intimidation is a powerful and unique fear. It is powerful because it alone can cause a man to sacrifice the opportunities of tomorrow for the status quo of yesterday. Intimidation brow-beats a man into deep feelings of inadequacy as his creativity, vision and might wilt before it. It is unique because it threatens our willingness to embrace God's future for our lives. All intimidation has to do is recite reality—it wants to disqualify you because you are not perfect. Intimidation starts those old tapes playing: *You are not smart or ingenious enough . . . you are not a great or even a good leader . . . you are ineffective and unfruitful . . . you have nothing in your past to suggest that you have it within you . . .* And on and on and on it goes. Intimidation goes so far as to use our heroes against us by reminding us that we can never be as good as those we idolize!

God's instructions to Joshua were not only for his battles—they are for our battles too! They do not reflect some kind of cute and novel whim on God's part. God intended that Joshua overcome Jericho and learn some principles that would empower him to live a faithful and fruitful life, unintimidated by what was before him. Let us learn these three tactics well:

> Walk around it . . . don't talk about it
> Sound your trumpet . . . don't beat your drum
> Shout . . . don't mumble or whisper[13]

Walk around it . . . don't talk about it. There will always be incongruity between the overwhelming proportion of the obstacle faced and the simple strategy and small stature of the one God calls. Here is an essential lesson: When the odds are stacked against you, don't talk about them.

One of my most painful experiences as a pastor came several years ago when I was wrongfully accused by leaders within my denomination of usurping the call of an interim pastor to the church I was serving as an associate pastor. I was called before a disciplinary committee and heard all kinds of falsehoods and innuendo. The meeting concluded with the chair stating that there was no place for me within our denomination. My response was to keep silent. I prayed for God to vindicate me by either removing those leaders from our district or by changing their hearts. Fourteen months later the chair of that committee and two others personally apologized—the other three had already moved. My silence paved the way for future leadership opportunities that would otherwise have remained inaccessible.

Through this I learned that the "strides of silence" have real impact:

1. *Silence deflates the tyranny of the obstacle before you.* In time, my life and conversations focused on other issues and relationships that did not intimidate me nor dominate my thinking. A faithful silence allowed me to see that my life was larger than the problem that wanted to overtake me. Silence gained me a higher ground to see that the Lord had other issues and opportunities that He considered more important than that with which I would naturally have chosen to be preoccupied.

2. *Silence protects you from saying words that may come back to compromise you.* You can neither understand the future nor completely perceive the motivations behind people's actions in the present. Words reflect our human vantage point. They underestimate God's power and provision while they overstate the impassibility of the obstacle before us. In my case, the disciplinary committee was acting on the falsehoods of one particular person. My silence gave them the emotional freedom to apologize later and kept me from uttering words I would someday regret.

3. *Silence fosters expectation and hope while it prepares you to see God's hand working on your behalf.* Silence forces your faith to be decisive— either you trust Him to lead, provide and overcome, or you do not. If you do, be quiet and follow Him; if you don't, then incessantly gossip, whine, complain and vent. We all know how the latter alternative is effective for tearing down strongholds and overcoming opposition!

Until next week . . .

Defeating Intimidation (Part 2)

Now Jericho was tightly shut. . . . The LORD said to Joshua, "See, I have given Jericho into your hand. . . . You shall march around the city, all the men of war circling the city once. You shall do so for six days. Also seven priests shall carry seven trumpets of rams' horns before the ark; then on the seventh day you shall march around the city seven times, and the priests shall blow the trumpets. . . . When you hear the sound of the trumpet, all the people shall shout with a great shout; and the wall of the city will fall down flat." (Joshua 6:1-5)

Recap of last week: Intimidation is a powerful and unique fear. . . . Intimidation is powerful because it alone can cause a man to sacrifice the opportunities of tomorrow for the status quo of yesterday. Intimidation browbeats a man into deep feelings of inadequacy as his creativity, vision and might wilt before it. Intimidation is unique because it threatens our willingness to embrace God's future for our lives. All intimidation has to do is recite reality—it wants to disqualify you because you are not perfect. . . . Intimidation goes so far as to use our heroes against us by reminding us that we can never be as good as those we idolize!

God showed Joshua three strategic tactics for overcoming obstacles and intimidation. Last week we examined the first one. (Walk around it . . . don't talk about it.) This week we'll look at the other two:

Sound your trumpet . . . don't beat your drum. In the Hebrew and Greek languages there is only one word for wind, breath and spirit because the biblical worldview depicts a recognition that our daily breath (our lives) requires God's breath (Holy Spirit) to be abundant, fruitful and victorious. Therefore I do not think God's instrumental preference is capricious or insignificant.

Whoever heard of an army who marched to the beat of trumpets as they went to battle?! Armies march to the beat of drums. Their beat establishes the pace of pursuit and their volume reflects the might of men. Trumpets, on the other hand, are brass instruments. Their primary role in Israel was to call people to praise, not to war. The message is clear: Spirit, not sweat, is the secret to overcoming intimidation and obstacles.

There is nothing like Holy Spirit-empowered praise in the face of intimidation and obstacles to focus our eyes on the One who holds everlasting victory in His hands.[14]

Shout . . . don't mumble or whisper. The Lord told Joshua in no uncertain terms, "When you hear the sound of the trumpet all the people shall shout with a great shout; and the wall of the city will fall down flat."

There is nothing vague or ambiguous here. God is not joking or playing juvenile games. He is not trying to concoct some kind of manly emotionalism. He is not asking for a vain display of triumphalism. He is calling them to shout on cue and in one accord so that Jericho might be "soundly" defeated. Three questions immediately come to mind.

1. *Why should we shout?* Because there are real walls that evil has intentionally built against us and there are invisible walls that sin has subtly fabricated within us. Both must come down. They will not come down through indifference or pious whisperings. God declares that there are some things that will only fall before the shout of His people.

2. *What should we shout?* A quick study of "shouting" in the Bible seems to indicate that we are to shout His praises, shout His triumphs and shout His graciousness that stands ready to bless. All three of these usually stand in marked contrast

to the pretenses, bluffs and power of the obstacles and intimidation we face.

3. *Do I really have to shout?* Yes! There is a season for silence (see last week!) and a season to shout. Our culture promotes the misguided notion that any display of spiritual emotion is foolish, fanatical and freakish. Thus we have adopted words like "reverent," "decorum" and "propriety" to justify our silence before a God who still recognizes the value of a good shout! The challenge is to be willing to shout, yet wise enough to wait for God's moment to do so.

There are Jerichos everywhere: fortified cities of doubt, fear, pride, strife, division, despair, hatred, poverty and prejudice. They exist within us and around us. Let us learn to apply God's Jericho strategy as we overcome our cultural apprehensions so that we may breach our adversary's walls. Now that will be something to shout about!

Until next week . . .

Closing in on God's Promises

> Then Caleb . . . said, "We should by all means go up and take possession of it, for we will surely overcome it." . . . But My servant Caleb, because he has had a different spirit and has followed Me fully, I will bring into the land which he entered, and his descendents shall take possession of it." (Numbers 13:30; 14:24)

> I [Caleb] was forty years old when Moses the servant of the LORD sent me . . . to spy out the land, and I brought word back to him as it was in my heart. . . . So Moses swore on that day, saying, "Surely the land on which your foot has trodden will be an inheritance to you and to your children forever." . . . Therefore, Hebron became the inheritance of Caleb . . . until this day, because he followed the LORD God of Israel fully. (Joshua 14:7, 9, 14)

Get up and break camp . . .

Gather manna . . .

Drink miracle water drawn from a rock . . .

Watch a pillar of cloud . . .
Spend the day wandering . . .
Set up camp . . .
Watch a pillar of fire and go to sleep . . .

That was then . . . but this is now.

Revile . . .
Up-and-at-'em . . .
Consecration . . .
Miracle crossings . . .
Sun standing still . . .
Miracle victories . . .
Momentum and vision . . .

Something changed . . . God's people were now taking Him at His Word.

Caleb is a man who wholeheartedly "closes in" to possess God's promised tomorrow. There is nothing casual about his desire to live faithfully. He is passionate, focused and intentional. His vision is not constrained by the limitations of yesterday or today. He sees his opportunities from the expansive vantage point of God's promises and confidently moves forward. Yet it is not Caleb's intensity but his ardent pursuit that delivers him safely into the land of God's promised tomorrows.

Caleb teaches us that there is a direct relationship between the pronouncement of God's promises to us and our own personal appropriation of those promises upon our lives. God's promises are not merely aphorisms to quote, but powerful kingdom certainties to embrace and by which we order our lives. Tomorrow's promises will never be realized by yesterday's old patterns. Instead, God's promises for tomorrow challenge us to live by tomorrow's patterns today.

While this inscription is personal, it is not private. God's promises are a catalyst for internal yet visible change as lives are reordered around the veracity and the certainty of His Word. Our lifestyle will increasingly reflect the substance of tomorrow's promises rather than today's uncertainties—and it will be evident for all to see.

Scripture indicates that the public reflection of your personal inscription of God's promises will include:

- Faithfully gathering with God's people to worship, pray and reflect upon His Word.
- Consecrating tithes and offerings in faithful giving to Him.
- Dedicating time, energy and creativity to loving service in Jesus' name.
- Confidently sharing the reality of God's love and presence in your life and in the world today with those who do not recognize Him yet.
- Deliberately working for reconciliation and overcoming barriers of prejudice and hostility.
- Firmly renouncing the exertion of demonic powers and sinful compromise in your life, relationships and surroundings.

You will not enter your "Promised Land" without change and a wholehearted pursuit of God.

Until next week . . .

Live in the Authority God Gave You

There are two kinds of people . . .
Both will look heavenward to the stars.
One will question why they appear to move as they do;
The other will command them to be still . . .

Now the Gibeonites, of all people, knew Joshua to be a man of his word. He rescued them from attack, as he had promised to do, but now he was faced with a strategic dilemma. God had not called him to merely put his enemies to flight; God had called Joshua to put his (His?) enemies to death in order to purify the land of a hostile, violent and tortuous paganism. Yet Joshua recognized that the noonday sun indicated that there would not be enough light to vanquish a scattered and confused opponent. There was only one thing to do . . .

> Joshua spoke to the LORD in the day when the LORD delivered up the Amorites before

the sons of Israel, and he said in the sight
of Israel,

"O sun, stand still at Gibeon,
    And O moon in the valley of Aijalon."
So the sun stood still, and the moon
        stopped,
Until the nation avenged themselves of
        their enemies. . . .

There was no day like that before it or after it, when the LORD listened to the voice
of a man; for the LORD fought for Israel.

Then Joshua and all Israel with him returned to the camp to Gilgal. (Joshua
10:12-15)

Commanding the sun to stand still in the sky
was as counterintuitive for Joshua as it would be
for us. Joshua recognized that he needed more
hours in the day to succeed (don't we all!), but
he failed to perceive that God had given him the
authority to succeed and triumph. Therefore it is
important to notice that Joshua spoke with the
Lord first and then as a result of that prayer put
his faith and leadership on the line by exercising
the authority that God had given him.

God did not simply place Joshua into a position
of authority; He endowed him with authority. The
same holds true for every Christian. Our calling is
not merely positional (i.e. where we stand before
God by His grace); our calling is also power-filled
because each of us is endowed with the Spirit of
God. God challenges us, like Joshua, not to step

back when our calling is incompatible with our circumstances. Instead He calls us to exercise our God-given authority amidst, and sometimes over, our circumstances so that we might remain focused on our calling and act consistently with it. For Joshua this meant that the only reasonable step of faith was to believe God for the unreasonable and the impossible!

In contrast to the courageous leadership faith inspires, we are privy to the cowardice that idolatry inspires. "Now the five kings [who had conspired together] had fled and hidden in the cave at Makkedah. . . . Joshua was told that the five kings had been found hiding in the cave at Makkedah" (10:16-17, NIV).

Joshua's pursuit of his enemy was temporarily distracted when he received news that the five kings who had inspired the attack on Gibeon were discovered hiding in a cave. While the people were content to call off the pursuit with such a prize in hand, Joshua was focused on his call—there was a battle to finish.

"Joshua said, 'Roll large stones against the mouth of the cave, and assign men by it to guard them, but do not stay there yourselves; pursue your enemies . . . for the LORD your God has delivered them into your hand' " (10:18-21).

After the battle, when Joshua returned triumphant, he commanded his people: " 'Open the mouth of the cave and bring these five kings out to me from the cave.' When they brought these kings out to Joshua, Joshua called for all the men of Israel, and said to the chiefs of the men of war who had gone with him, 'Come near, put your feet on the necks of these kings' " (10:22, 24).

The next verse gives the reason for this unusual command: "Joshua then said to them, 'Do not fear or be dismayed! Be strong and courageous, for thus the LORD will do to all your enemies with whom you fight' " (10:25).

Joshua was exhorting his men, through this object lesson, to live with a faith that was consistent with the authority God had given them—a lesson he had just (re)learned! What a graphic and rich illustration to convict the people of God with! Our God gives His people, regardless of rank or stature, the authority to trample kings under their feet!

The Scriptures teach us that whatever is "brought under foot" is defeated, vanquished and brought under dominion. When Jesus said to His disciples, "Behold, I have given you authority to tread on serpents and scorpions, and over all the power of the enemy, and nothing will injure you" (Luke 10:19), He wasn't proposing some new ritual akin to fire-walking. He was declaring that they (and all believers after them) were endowed with authority over all the power of the enemy. Therefore we, of all people, are free to be courageous as God strengthens us with the truth of His promises.[15]

The foundation for this authority is rooted in the throne Jesus occupies:

> [God] raised Him from the dead and
> seated Him at His right hand in the
> heavenly places, far above all rule and
> authority and power and dominion, and
> every name that is named, not only in
> this age but also in the one to come. And
> He put all things in subjection under His
> feet. . . . (Ephesians 1:20-22)

We will not possess our tomorrows if we do not learn to live in the authority God has given us today. Possessing tomorrow will not go uncontested. It is the nature of hostile kings (demonic and human) to resist, attack and boast against everything God has done, wants to do and will do. Therefore let the Holy Spirit strengthen you with this powerful promise:

You will never be disabled from successfully resisting and overcoming the ones who contest against the call and work of God in your life.

Until next week . . .

Beware of Complacency!

Poverty and affluence alike test the soul—albeit from opposite ends of the spectrum. We may cry out amidst poverty, "My God, why have You forgotten me?" But God may cry out to us amidst our affluence, "My child, why have you forgotten Me?" Both sift the soul, looking for responsive obedience, sincere gratitude and a confident trust in the promises of God.

> It came about when the sons of Israel became strong, they put the Canaanites to forced labor, but they did not drive them out completely. . . . So Joshua said to the sons of Israel, "How long will you put off entering to take possession of the land which the LORD, the God of your fathers, has given you?" (Joshua 17:13; 18:3)

Aphorisms abound: "Don't grow weary in well-doing"; "Good things come to those who wait." In Joshua's case it had taken forty-five years to fulfill God's promise that the family of Israel would possess the land God had sworn to Moses. At the seasoned age of eighty-five, Joshua begins to divide up the Promised Land among the twelve tribes so they might possess their possession. He recognizes that there are still hostile tribal remnants that need to be defeated. However, he also understands that they pose no strategic threat to the distribution of the land according to God's promise to His people.

Yet among the tedious real estate records describing the divisions of land (13:1-22:9), Joshua issues a prophetic challenge to the nation: "How long will you fail to take possession of your possession?" They had failed to take complete hold of the land that God had given them, although their land stretched out before them.

Had God lost His power?
    Had God reneged on His promises?
        Was He unwilling to keep His Word?
            Had He laid aside His commands issued for their safety, security and success?
    Had He excused Himself from the scene?
Why, then, did they not confidently move forward?

The bottom line is that they grew complacent. "Enough already . . . we've won . . . we're here . . . we're strong . . . let's be practical . . ." And so they, who had been slaves, enslaved a people because they wanted peace and prosperity. For the sake of ease and money they deliberately chose not to "possess their tomorrows" and instead enslaved themselves and others in the sinful patterns of their "yesterdays" (slavery in Egypt).

There is a challenging kingdom warning here for God's beloved. It is possible for us to enter our possession without possessing it for our own because we choose to stray from the lifeline of God's promises. At issue is not the security of our salvation in Christ but the actualization of the powerful promises of God within the life and community of a believer. These promises can shape our destiny if we will surrender ourselves to them and live consistently by them.

In Christ we have been promised more than land—we have been promised a kingdom. Yet, like our ancestors, we make our peace with what is unclean in our land because we desire peace, ease, comfort and greater wealth. Jesus cautioned that some of God's beloved would bring "no fruit to maturity" because they are choked with worries, riches and the pleasures of this life (Luke 8:14).

Israel's failure to temporarily forego peace and prosperity in order to hold fast to God's promises sowed the seeds for future compromise, heartache, loss, grief and division. Their families for generations to come lived under God's love amidst the conflicting circumstances that their forebears created for them.

Be strong and courageous—do not fear! Cleanse your land of "Canaanites" and do not make peace with sin in your borders. Then you

will enter and possess the kingdom God has be-
queathed to you.

Until next week . . .

Fidelity and Unity Are Inseparable

All Israel was outraged, betrayed and frightened. The last time something similar to this happened, God judged them with a severe plague that killed thousands. This time they had determined to be resolute—never again would they allow this offense to go uncontested (Joshua 22:10-20). Now is the time to take action. Now is the time to call the men to war. There was no time for diplomatic councils and conversations. The generals would be the diplomats and overwhelming military force would be the "finer points" of their diplomatic presentation.

The cause of this crisis was simple. The tribes east of the Jordan (Rueben, Gad and Manasseh) had constructed an enormous and impressive altar that could be seen from everywhere. The leaders of Israel were certain that this was an act of hubris and rebellion. It appeared to them that the eastern tribes intended to establish their own "worship center" east of the Jordan, forsake the Tabernacle at Bethel and worship the pagan gods of the Caananites.

Every crisis needs a cause, but beware: Looks can be deceiving.

When the armies of Israel confronted the eastern tribes, they discovered that their outrage was completely unfounded. Instead of idolatry, they discovered a passionate fidelity that evidenced the nobility and singular commitment of a people that desired to remain true to God and united with all His people.

> "The Mighty One, God, the LORD, the Mighty One, God, the LORD! He knows, and may Israel itself know. If it was in rebellion, or if in an unfaithful act against the LORD do not save us this day! If we have built us an altar to turn away from following the LORD, or if to offer a burnt offering or grain offering on it, or if to offer sacrifices of peace offerings on it, may the LORD Himself require it. But truly we have done this out of concern, for a reason, saying, 'In time to come your sons may say to our sons, "What have you to do with the LORD, the God of Israel?' . . . Therefore we said, 'Let us build an altar, not for burnt offering or for sacrifice; rather it shall be a witness between us and you and between our generations after us.'" (22:22-24, 26-27)

There is a timeless and essential kingdom principle here: Fidelity and unity are inseparable. Authentic worship and credible righteousness necessitate a steadfast commitment to and involvement with the congregation of God's people.

Church membership is a vulnerable and realistic admission of spiritual need and a hunger for community. Twice-born people (see John 3:3) need a family's love just as much as a just-born child. But this hunger will never be satiated if the same apathy and impermanence we see in the world around us should mark our relationships in the church. In membership I confess that I need a church family that provides prayer support, corrective admonition, godly examples, an encouraging word, prophetic insight, an equipping hand and a sending purpose.

Church membership is not an unspiritual capitulation to the last remaining vestiges of dead ecclesiastical institutionalism. It is a deliberate commitment, catalyzed by the Holy Spirit, which displays a royal loyalty that confesses:

I am a member of the King's family. I know in what house He has placed me. Therefore let

my presence in His house;
 my participation with His people;
  my persistent commitment to His call; and
   my passion to serve His loved ones reflect
   my identity as one accepted and adopted;
  my gratitude for His love and saving hand;
 my surrender to His authority and commands;
and my love for His larger body, the Church.

Until next week . . .

Your Battles Are the Lord's

Now it came about after many days, when the LORD had given rest to Israel from all their enemies on every side, and Joshua was old, advanced in years, that Joshua called for all Israel, for their elders and their heads and their judges and their officers, and said to them, "I am old, advanced in years. And you have seen all that the LORD your God has done to all these nations because of you, for the LORD your God is He who has been fighting for you."
(Joshua 23:1-3)

oshua's farewell address to Israel is more than the sage words of a godly leader intended to inspire a nation. This is no mere reflection on victories won and ground gained. In this speech you will not find the self-congratulatory banter of troops who, after fighting side by side, revel in their triumph.

This is the final message, one last good-bye, from a beloved leader to his people because he knows his death is imminent (Joshua 23:1). It is the passionate charge of a godly man and a commanding leader whose eye remains on the future. Therefore his strategic intent is to inspire his people to remain faithful to the Lord so that they may bequeath their victory, blessings and gain to each succeeding generation. Joshua's farewell message forms a foundation for every child of God who desires to faithfully possess his tomorrows, freely embrace his todays and impart a lasting legacy of faithfulness.

Joshua publicly acknowledged and praised God for the victories they had experienced together under God's leadership (23:3). Joshua's speech is not about Joshua—it is about the Lord. Remarkably absent is any recitation of personal accomplishment or self-serving praise. Joshua truly believed that Israel's victories came solely from God's leadership and not from his own. His lifestyle of praise equipped those around him to understand that their present well-being and future security was found in God and not in his own loving leadership. True and transforming victory comes only from the hand of God. Wise is the man who understands this. Thankful is the man who experiences this. Faithful is the man who declares it.

Joshua testified to God's faithfulness to honor every promise He has made (23:14). While Joshua's integrity cultivated respect for the authority God had anointed him with, it is important to recognize that he did absolutely nothing to establish a personality cult that would be dependent upon his every whim, wish or word. Joshua went out of his way to develop a worldview that perceived well-being, peace and triumph as signs of God's covenant faithfulness rather than his own wisdom and ingenuity. Joshua was committed to making this a nation that was independently dependent on God and not on any single individual. Joshua's example imparted the understanding that the security and hope of Israel were rooted in God's faithfulness to uphold His promises and not in her mortal leadership.

Joshua declared that God's promises would ensure their future victories (23:10). Whenever the people of God forget or neglect the promises of God, they are treading on precarious soil because they will usually turn to the spiritual counterfeits of God's promises—power, prestige and/or personal gain. These are counterfeits because they provide inspiration, focus and vision for living—just like God's promises—but they are birthed in selfishness, fear and a godless will to power. They inspire idolatry rather than faithfulness and therefore they are costly to the souls of the men in whom they reside. Such men are self-serving rather than God-serving. They become takers and users rather than servers and givers. Such men may pride themselves on their spirituality, but in fact their faith has meaning only to the extent that it satisfies their wants and feeds their desires.

Is it not instructive that the book of Judges introduces an era of compromise and faithlessness with these words: "Then Joshua the son of Nun, the servant of the LORD, died. . . . All that generation also were gathered to their fathers; and there arose another generation after them who did not know the LORD, nor yet the work which He had done for Israel" (Judges 2:8, 10)? They were ignorant because they chose to forget, not because they had not been instructed.

There is never a time when the child of God does not need his faith buttressed by God's promises for the future. Life is dynamic, not static—despite the attempts by some to control everything! Each day we face sin's *troika*—the world, the flesh and the devil. Their assaults are as endless as the ongoing campaigns against Israel by her enemies. Tomorrow's insecurities and disappointments may quickly unseat today's triumphs. Therefore, God promises that He will fight for us and deliver us safely if we will cling to Him and order our lives under His authority. The person whose mind is fastened on God's promises for his future will not act precipitously in the present because he understands that God's promises have already secured his future today.

E N D N O T E S

1. This reflection was inspired by Elijah P. Brown, "The Wonderful Teacher," quoted in *The Jesus Book*, ed. Calvin Miller (New York: Simon and Schuster, 1996), pp. 111-113.

2. These five statements are not original to me, although I have slightly modified the fifth affirmation. I heard them recited by Joseph Garlington, who indicated that they were from a congregation in Costa Rica.

3. I heard this interpretation first from Michael Green who was then serving as Vicar at St. Aldates Church, Oxford, England.

4. J.I. Packer, *Evangelism and the Sovereignty of God* (Downers Grove, IL: Intervarsity Press, 1991), p. 108.

5. A.W. Tozer, *How to Be Filled with the Holy Spirit* (Camp Hill, PA: Christian Publications, n.d.), pp. 43-46.

6. A.B. Simpson, "I Take, He Undertakes," *Hymns of the Christian Life* (Camp Hill, PA: Christian Publications, 1978), #290.

7. I am grateful to Ed Beach, a member of our Leadership Team (elder) for this insight drawn from years of being a tender, wise and fruitful gardener.

8. These are adapted from the three steps of integrity suggested by Stephen Carter in his book, *Integrity* (New York: Basic Books, 1995). Carter is a Christian who teaches constitutional law at Yale. While one may not agree with his positions, his writing is thoughtful and worthy of our interaction.

9. A.W. Tozer, *The Price of Neglect* (Camp Hill, PA: Christian Publications, 1991), p. 12.

10. Jack Canfield and Mark Victor Hansen, *Chicken Soup for the Soul* (Deerfield Beach, FL: Health Communications, 1993), pp. 236-237.

11. Excerpted from Jim Cymbala, *Fresh Wind, Fresh Fire* (Grand Rapids, MI: Zondervan, 1997), pp. 170-173.

12. C.S. Lewis, *Mere Christianity* (New York: Regal Books, 1989), p. 55f.

13. My pastoral understanding of Joshua has been shaped by the teachings of Jack Hayford. These three points are adapted from his book, *Taking Hold of Tomorrow* (Ventura, CA: Regal Books, 1989), pp. 109-127.

14. Excerpted from Jack Hayford, *Taking Hold of Tomorrow* (Ventura, CA: Regal Books, 1989), pp. 122-123.

15. Ibid., p. 186.